# THE NORWEGIAN SYNOD
## 1853-1917

A Short History of a
Premier Predecessor Church Body

O. ROLF OLSON

Lutheran University Press
Minneapolis, Minnesota

The Norwegian Synod, 1853-1917
*A Short History of a Premier Predecessor Church Body*
by O. Rolf Olson

Copyright 2016 O. Rolf Olson. All rights reserved. Published by Lutheran University Press, an imprint of 1517 Media. Except for breif quotations in critical articles or reviews, no part of this book may be reproduced in any manner without prior written permission from the publisher.

ISBN: 978-1-942304-18-0
eISBN: 978-1-942304-88-3

The cover includes images of key leaders and locations for the Norwegian Synod (clockwise, starting at top right): J. W. C. Dietrichson, who initiated the first move to organize congregations into a church body; Laur. Larsen, who was the president of Luther College from its beginning and served as editor of church publications; P. A. Rasmussen, who pioneered mission outreach for the Synod; H. G. Stub, president of the Norwegian Synod at the Grand Union in 1917; C. K. Preus, president of Luther College after Larsen and leader in theological discussion toward the Grand Union; Old Main at Luther College, one of the premier educational institutions of the Synod; H. A. Preus, long-time president, pastor, and leader of the Synod; U. V. Koren, pioneer leader and theologian; B. J. Muus, founder of St. Olaf College; the original Washington Prairie church building, one of the first in the synod.

This book is dedicated to the honor and memory
of three Norwegian Synod stalwarts,
who also served well into the Synod's successor church body,
the Norwegian Lutheran Church in America/
Evangelical Lutheran Church:

Dr. Oscar L. Olson, my paternal grandfather,
president of Luther College and professor of English

The Rev. Kristen R. Kvamme, my maternal grandfather,
parish pastor, hymn writer, and city missionary

The Rev. Dr. T. F. Gullixson, my great uncle,
president of Luther Theological Seminary, parish pastor,
and vice president of the
Norwegian Lutheran Church in America/
Evangelical Lutheran Church

# Table of Contents

Introduction ................................................................................. 7

Foreword .................................................................................... 10

CHAPTER ONE
The False Start and the Bona Fide Start ............................................. 11

CHAPTER TWO
The Immediate History of the Synod Following Organization ............ 19

CHAPTER THREE
Founding Pastors of the Synod ......................................................... 25

CHAPTER FOUR
The Polity of the Synod Revised ....................................................... 31

CHAPTER FIVE
Membership in the Synodical Conference ......................................... 34

CHAPTER SIX
The Slavery Issue ............................................................................. 36

CHAPTER SEVEN
Inter-Synodical Theological and Doctrinal Discussions ...................... 44

CHAPTER EIGHT
Publications ..................................................................................... 51

CHAPTER NINE
Worship and Church Music .............................................................. 55

CHAPTER TEN
The Election Controversy ................................................................. 58

CHAPTER ELEVEN
Home Missions Before the Election Controversy (1864-1887) .......... 77

CHAPTER TWELVE
Home Missions After the Election Controversy (1890-1917) ............ 82

CHAPTER THIRTEEN
The Synod's Education Enterprise ..................................................... 89

CHAPTER FOURTEEN
The Synod and Foreign Missions ...................................................... 97

CHAPTER FIFTEEN
Social Ministry Institutions .............................................................. 109

CHAPTER SIXTEEN
The Union Movement in the Synod ................................................. 115

CHAPTER SEVENTEEN
An Evaluation of the Norwegian Synod ............................................ 152

APPENDIX
Synod Membership ......................................................................... 156

Sources ............................................................................................ 157

Bibliography .................................................................................... 159

# Introduction

Of all the predecessor church bodies of the current Evangelical Lutheran Church in America (ELCA), the Norwegian Synod (1853-1917) was arguably the most theologically confessional. During the time of its tenure confessionalism gave this church body a unique status among all Lutheran church bodies. Almost one century later its confessionalism remains a unique contribution to the ELCA of the present time.

The Synod (as it will henceforth be named) was one of the best organized pioneer church bodies in America. In contrast to some of its sister bodies, the Synod was carefully, competently, and meticulously organized from its beginning. It was precise and effective in its ecclesiastical procedure. Its structure became a model for several successor Lutheran church organizations.

The Synod was privileged to have possibly the most capable and best-educated leadership of any pioneer church body. Remarkably, ten of its first eleven pastors and founders had been university-educated in Norway. All of these eleven leaders were high-quality individuals, who became noteworthy frontier pastors. Their congregations and constituencies adored them for generations following their service. The high standards of clergy education and individual personal quality remained benchmarks for pastoral leadership throughout the Synod's history. In this respect, too, the Synod remains a model for the absolute significance that capable and well-educated leadership can give to the church.

The Synod became a founder of lasting institutions. A theological seminary, several colleges, strong congregations, many charitable organizations and institutions, and vibrant overseas mission fields (which after many years became indigenous church bodies) are part of its current and up-to-date legacy.

The Synod from its beginning was itself the heir of a strong contemporary spiritual awakening in Norway. The Haugean Revival had re-vitalized church members, clergy, and theological faculties alike. In addition, many Norwegian Lutheran theologians had been the heirs of a then-current renaissance of German Lutheran confessionalism. Much of the direct influence on the Synod had come from the awakened-influenced professors at the University of Oslo (Christiania in those days), who were the teachers and mentors of the Synod's early clergy.

In contrast with much of Norwegian-American Lutheranism, the Synod was liturgical, purposefully confessional, clergy-led, church-oriented in its piety, and education-emphasizing with its membership. All these qualities are vital parts of its heritage.

The Synod was also strongly ecumenical—within the ranks of Lutheranism. For most of its existence it was closely aligned with the Missouri Synod. For over a decade it was a member of the Synodical Conference. It always reached out to fellow Lutherans, especially those of its common ethnic (Norwegian) background. It longed for unity with these groups, but insisted such unity be strongly confessional in nature. The highest standards were maintained for ecumenical and inter-synodical fellowship. In its ecumenical aspirations it set a standard for modern inter-church efforts.

The Synod did concentrate and excel in the field of education at all levels: parish, secondary, collegiate, theological, and professional. This is a major gift in itself.

Another area of excellence was evangelism and home missions. The Synod's outreach and growth were phenomenal. Most pastors and many others played a role in this endeavor. Outreach set the pace for successor groups in this priority area, which continues to modern times.

In the fields of social services and charities, the Synod admitted to a slow start. However, the seeds were always present in the Synod's life. Care for the unfortunate, the deprived, the distressed, and the needy was part-and-parcel of the Synod's membership. In the lead-up to the Civil War, Synod people took strong exception to the degrading institution of slavery. During the war they staunchly supported the Union cause. Once organized social services were begun, the Synod made a significant contribution.

The Synod took great pains to keep its membership informed. It would do so through two means: a highly developed parish education program and outstanding publications. Information and education gave the Synod's congregations and membership unique strength. In both of these areas the Synod was a forerunner and role model for current church-wide education programs.

Although the Synod was consistently and competently led by the clergy, amazingly the lay membership always had the last word. (This "last word" phenomenon was in part the result of the Synod's strenuous efforts at lay education and dissemination of information.) Synod decisions and actions required lay approval, and sometimes the laity modified or altered the final result. The congregations were democratically organized; and the synodical organization (starting with hierarchy) became increasingly democratic as time moved on.

Finally, the Synod played a major role in preparation for the Grand Union of 1917. It made plans to merge its life with other Norwegian Lutheran church bodies to form the Norwegian Lutheran Church in America (NLCA). This effort was a forerunner to two more comprehensive Lutheran mergers later in the twentieth century. Much of the Synod's emphasis and leadership has influenced American Lutheranism to the present day.

# Foreword

The major activity and ministry of the Synod for the Norwegian Evangelical Lutheran Church took place in its congregations and institutions. However, the purpose of this volume is to focus on the synodical organization itself as well as its activities and actions. Many congregational and institutional histories have been written for their own constituencies. In most cases, these accounts have been rendered very well. This is intended to look at the larger scope of the Norwegian Synod's work.

The Synod organization and function is a story in itself, and a very engaging one at that. This effort will touch on the various entities within the synodical organization only to the extent that they bear directly on the Synod itself.

The historical background of the Synod, preceding its organization—via ethnic immigration and congregational organization—also will not be treated here. The first attempt to organize the Synod itself will be the starting point of this narrative. The actual establishment of the Synod took place exactly ten years after the founding of the first Norwegian-American Lutheran congregation. This volume covers the life of the Synod, both positive and negative aspects, until it merges with two sister church bodies to become something larger than itself. Special note is taken of the Synod's lasting effects and permanent influences.

This account is definitely a composite. Many secondary sources and many records have been consulted. The objective of the narrative is to arrive at a comprehensive and total account of the sixty-four years of the Synod for the Norwegian Evangelical Lutheran Church.

CHAPTER ONE

# The False Start and the Bona Fide Start

It would take five conventions to organize the Norwegian Synod. This would be an indication of how carefully, meticulously, and properly organized this church body would be.

Pioneer Pastor Johannes Wilhelm Christian (J. W. C.) Dietrichson, who served at Koshkonong (1844-1850), was the original leader in synod formulation. As early as 1847 he had conferred with Pastor Claus Lauritz Clausen, the first pastor at Muskego (the first Norwegian-American Lutheran congregation, organized in 1843), about the possibility of a theological seminary. Both agreed that it would have to await a synodical organization.

Dietrichson was a capable organizer of many congregations and a real servant of the church. He did excellent work in the short run. However, he did have an authoritarian personality which did not fit him for the frontier in the long run. But he was the first to see the need for a united organization of congregations. And it was Dietrichson who produced the draft constitution which became the basic document for the Synod constitution throughout its history.

The very first attempt to organize a church body, or synod of congregations, took place in 1849. Dietrichson took the initiative. When Pastor Hans Andreas(H. A.) Stub arrived from Norway, Dietrichson approached him with the idea of forming a synod. Both Stub and Clausen supported Dietrichson's proposal.

In April, 1949, Dietrichson issued a call to the congregations, inviting them to send delegates to a meeting at Koshkonong on July 15, 1849. Unfortunately, Dietrichson's authoritarian and abrasive personality defeated the very worthy plan; he had already offended too many pioneer church people. An effective quorum was not present; only Dietrichson and a few scattered delegates actually showed up.

The next year, in 1850, Dietrichson returned permanently to Norway.

## The First Convention

With the arrival of Pastor Adolph Carl(A. C.) Preus, from Norway, at Koshkonong in 1850, the hopes of a new synod were re-activated. Pastors Preus, Stub, and Clausen launched a new effort in 1850 to bring the congregations together.

On December 5, 1850, the formal notice was publicized for a meeting just after the New Year 1851, at Luther Valley, Wisconsin. The meeting was held January 5-9, 1851. Pastors Stub, Clausen, and Preus plus thirty delegates from eighteen congregations were in attendance. Only four invited congregations did not attend.

Pastor A. C. Preus was elected chairman. A constitutional draft was presented; it was undoubtedly the same document prepared by Dietrichson before he returned to Norway. The chief debate was not on the contents of the draft constitution; the debate was over the name. The name chosen, out of several proposals, was the one suggested by Preus: "The Norwegian Evangelical Lutheran Church in America." (Note the similarity to the name of the current ELCA.)

Following convention discussion, a constitution of twelve paragraphs and seventeen bylaws was adopted.

Clausen made a special motion that the doctrine of conversion after death be discarded. This motion was adopted, thus preventing this issue from ever becoming a part of the Synod.

Disagreement did develop, however, over the election of a synodical superintendent and a church council before the official acceptance of the constitution by the congregations. Nonetheless, it was decided to proceed with the election, so that the Synod could function in the meantime. Clausen, the pastor of the host congregation (he was now pastor at Luther Valley), was elected superintendent. Preus was elected vice-superintendent. Four lay members were elected to the council; this gave the lay members a two-thirds majority on the six-member council. And a resolution was passed that the Second Convention meet at Muskego in February 1852.

In the meantime, action on the constitution was to be reported by the congregations before the third Wednesday in May, when the newly-elected council was to hold its first meeting.

There is no evidence that any such reports were received from the congregations. This lack of evidence may have indicated lay fears of clergy domination. It is clear throughout the First Convention at Luther Valley in January there had been evidence that the lay delegates—especially the Muskego delegation—had been sensitive to the possibility of clergy control. It is significant that Clausen (always sensitive to lay feeling) included in his pamphlet on the constitution a statement that adequate safeguards against dominance by the pastors had been provided.

## The Second Convention

Clergy opposition to the constitution developed almost immediately with the arrival of three new pastors from Norway: G. F. Dietrichson, a cousin of J. W. C. Dietrichson's father and a brother-in-law of A. C. Preus; Hermann Amberg (H. A.) Preus, a cousin of A. C. Preus; and Nils Brandt.

Dietrichson became pastor at Luther Valley. (Clausen had resigned because of ill health, while still serving a small congregation at Wiota.) H. A. Preus was the new pastor at Spring Prairie. Brandt was to serve Rock River and Pine Lake.

The coming of these three men re-shaped the movement toward synodical organization. Although these pastors arrived too late to attend the First Convention at Luther Valley in 1851, they immediately made known their opposition to the constitution.In spite of the general agreement at the First Convention in January 1851, there were statements in the constitution which were unacceptable to them.

Paragraph Two defined church doctrine as "revealed through God's holy word in our baptismal covenant as well as in the canonical books of the Old and New Testaments." This was unmistakably an expression of Grundtvigianism, which tended to place the baptismal covenant (of the Apostles' Creed) above the Scriptures as the criterion of Christian teaching. To this these three new pastors were uncompromisingly opposed. When the Second Convention was held at Muskego on February 1-9, 1852, the delegates were promptly faced with a motion by A. C. Preus (H. A. Preus, Dietrichson, and Brandt were present but not yet members of the church body) to regard the actions of the First Convention of 1851 "as mere preliminary motions" and to "join with the pastors and the delegates from the congregations that have not yet joined the synod, in order to review and test the synodical constitution."

The unanimous adoption of this motion had the effect of declaring the enactments of the First Convention of 1851 to be null and void. The result of this action was that Grundtvigianism never prevailed in the Synod—or in any branch of Norwegian-American Lutheranism. Doctrinal concern was evident from the beginning of the Synod, even before it had been fully established.

## The Third Convention

When the act of dissolution had been made, the Third Convention was immediately called and convened in place. Now the three new pastors and their congregations were received—making the total attendance six pastors and thirty-seven delegates from twenty-one congregations.

Clausen immediately withdrew as presiding officer in order that a new election could be held. He was the sole pastor in the group who did not hold a university degree—and the only non-Norwegian present. He seemed to be very self-conscious about his unique status.

The assembly then elected A. C. Preus president and Clausen vice president. It considered and acted upon several items of business, including the decision to submit its actions to the congregations for approval. Several of the questions discussed on the floor indicated the breadth of interests among the churchmen. A. C. Preus and Clausen were concerned about church union. Preus urged closer affiliation with the Joint Synod of Ohio (which was German), with the prospect of utilizing Capital University at Columbus for ministerial education. Clausen's interest was mostly nationalistic; he felt everything should be done to bring about a united Norwegian Lutheranism. The question of ministerial supply, according to Dietrichson, should be faced by electing a committee of pastors to procure ordained men from Norway to accept assignments in America. H. A. Preus saw the need for a committee on temporary church government to care for interim problems and to issue a call for the next convention.

With these preliminary discussions concluded, the convention gave its attention to the main item of business, the review of the constitution. Immediately H. A. Preus moved that the words "in our baptismal covenant" be eliminated from Paragraph Two. All but Clausen voted for the motion; Clausen maintained that the original expressed his conviction. (Clausen remained a Grundtvigian, but only a mild Grundtvigian.) With this major change made, the constitution and bylaws with minor alterations were ready to be submitted to the congregations for study and suggestions

Committee reports and the passing of resolutions completed the business of the convention:

1) A high-profile item was the report on union with the Joint Synod of Ohio. The invitation to affiliate had been extended by President William Reynolds of Capital University. The invitation was courteously declined because of the preparatory nature of the present convention and the lack of information regarding the Joint Synod.

2) Resolutions were adopted promoting Christian living among the members by the urging of family devotions, discipline, religious schools, and good literature.

3) Resolutions were also passed frowning on and urging refraining from such practices as "night-hawking," dancing, gambling, drinking, etc. The problems of the frontier were reflected in items two and three

4) A committee on interim affairs was charged with calling the next convention.

With the adjournment of the Third Convention, the "False Start" of the Norwegian Synod would come to its conclusion. Congregational study of the proposed constitution and the Fourth Convention would be preparation for the Fifth Convention, which would actually serve as the Constituting Convention.

## The Fourth Convention

Before the actual organization of the Synod, the group of university-educated pastors was augmented by the arrival in 1852 of another minister, Jacob Aal Ottesen. The young clergyman, like his friends from Norway, was an advocate of strong confessional Lutheranism. He arrived in time to add his weight to the growing confessional party. Following the two Muskego conventions of 1852, this group was to lead the emerging Synod.

The Fourth Convention, meeting at East Koshkonong, was called by the interim committee on church government and began its work on February 3, 1853. No fewer than nineteen alterations to the constitution and bylaws were laid before the convention by the congregations. After an examination and discussion of the changes, the constitution was ready for final submission to the congregations.

Those congregations who approved the document were to send delegates to a constituting convention at Luther Valley on October 3-7, 1853, at which time the Synod would be formally organized. The fifth organizational convention would then be the actual Constituting Convention.

## The Fifth Convention

The Constituting Convention was held on October 3-7, 1853, and the Norwegian Synod began to function in October 1853 as a fully-organized church body with a constitution and permanent officers.

Six pastors and delegates from seventeen congregations were present. The six pastors were A. C. Preus, H. A. Preus, G.F. Dietrichson, Nils Brandt, H. A. Stub, and J. A. Ottesen. The seventh pastor, C. L. Clausen, was absent.

The two Preuses, Dietrichson, and Brandt had guided their congregations into the organization. Stub had been unable to quiet his Muskego congregation's fear of hierarchy; and so Muskego remained outside the Synod for the indefinite future. Ottesen (newly arrived and also present) had too recently come upon the scene to have established regularly-functioning congregations.

Clausen was a conspicuous absence. He had recently moved from Luther Valley to St. Ansgar, Iowa. A veteran of ten years (1843-1853) service on the frontier, Clausen (for reasons of health) had temporarily given up pastoral work. He had, however, maintained an active interest in synodical negotiations. Yet it was Clausen's former parish at Luther Valley which became the birthplace of the Norwegian Evangelical Lutheran Church of America.

The constitution that had been so painstakingly prepared by J. W. C. Dietrichson in 1849 had been adopted in 1851, annulled in 1852, revised in 1852, revised again in February 1853, and finally adopted again in October 1853. It was a carefully worked out instrument of church polity. It sought carefully to adapt the spirit and practice of the Church of Norway to the American frontier.

It should be noted that the doctrinal position of the new church body was that of the 1851 constitution with its Grundtvigianism expunged. In keeping with the Dano-Norwegian Lutheran state church tradition, only the Augsburg Confession and Luther's Small Catechism were specified as confessional requirements, in addition to the Ecumenical Creeds.

The liturgy of the Danish-Norwegian Church of 1685 was adopted as the order of worship—with the understanding that the Synod might alter it.

The structure of this new church body was to be "synodical-presbyterial," with the highest authority vested in the synod, which was to meet bi-annually. The explanation of "synodical-presbyterial" was to be found in the original document of 1849, in which Dietrichson explains the phrase by stating that "the synod shall elect a Presbyterium or a Church Council" to have responsibility for church matters between meetings of the synod. The duties of the church council included (1) disciplinary supervision of the pastors, (2) the responsibility of making initial judgments in all religious-ecclesiastical matters, and (3) the authority to call extraordinary meetings of the synod when necessary. In other words, the polity was definitely "high church," following the pattern of the Church of Norway.

The powers of the Synod were described by Dietrichson as follows:

1) to provide general and specific rules governing all religious-ecclesiastical matters,
2) to be the final judge (even to over-ruling the church council) in all matters,
3) to elect a president from among the pastors of the church, and
4) to choose a church council of three clergy and three lay members.

The president—besides being the presiding officer—was charged with carrying out all rules, decisions, and judgments of the church council.

The Constituting Convention (which the Synod would regard as the first of its many general conventions) elected the following men to executive offices:

President: A. C. Preus

Clergy members of the church council: A. C. Preus, H. A. Preus, and G. F. Dietrichson

Lay members of the church council: I. Ingebretson, L. J. Lee, and J. O. Fosmark.

The constitution weighed the balance of authority in favor of the Synod rather than the congregations. It reflected the polity of the Church of Norway with its emphasis on hierarchical government. It definitely reflected the background of all these pioneer churchmen, and especially the pastors who had been university-educated.

The over-emphasis on hierarchy to the short-changing of congregational authority would be recognized later in the constitutional revisions of 1867-68 and 1874-76. But, by and large, the polity of 1853 continued to be the framework in which all the work of the Synod would be done for the next sixty-four years—the length of the Synod's tenure.

The False Start and the Bona Fide Start | 17

The organization of the Synod was a crowning achievement and success. It combined the confessions and practices of the Church of Norway with a well-ordered free church on American soil. The entire organization was remarkably articulated and carefully provided for in the constitution of 1853.

### Synod Statistics at the Time of Its Founding

Pastors: Seven

Congregations: Thirty-eight

Members: 11,400 (estimated)

CHAPTER TWO

# The Immediate History of the Synod Following Organization

The Norwegian Synod rapidly assumed a position of pre-eminence among Norwegian-American Lutheran church groups. Only the Eielsen Synod, founded in 1846, had preceded it. (The Eielsen Synod would be re-organized in 1876 to form Hauge's Synod.)

During the next twenty-five years, to 1878, the Synod grew in size and influence, cultivated contacts with other confessional Lutheran bodies, built schools, published papers, and engaged in dialogue (even controversy) with other church and secular groups.

During these years the Synod flourished. Even though it was feared and attacked on all sides because of its immediate prominence, it successfully countered its opposition. Those who took exception to the Synod did so because it was perceived to advocate institutional and staunchly confessional Christianity. It emerged with strength from these encounters.

In the meantime more outstanding men would arrive from Norway during the 1850s, in the wake of the Synod's organization: Ulrik Vilhelm Koren, who arrived in 1853, would become the chief theologian and chief literary defender of the Synod's theological position; Peter Laurentius (Laur.) Larsen, who arrived in 1857, become the first president of Luther College and the long-term editor-in-chief of Synod publications; Bernt Julius Muus, who arrived in 1859, become the Synod's chief loyal dissenter and the founder of St. Olaf College.

## Affiliation with the Missouri Synod

The general position the Synod assumed and defended was supported by the Synod's co-operation with and strong alliance with the Missouri Synod.

In the 1850s there were two prominent Lutheran church bodies on the American scene:

1) The General Synod of the Evangelical Lutheran Church. Organized in 1820, this body was known for its weak confessional theological position. Norwegian Lutherans as a whole, and the Synod in particular, viewed this wing of American Lutheranism with profound suspicion. This attitude on the part of Norwegian-American Lutherans would last well over a century.

2) The German Evangelical Lutheran Synod of Missouri, Ohio, and Other States—commonly known as the Missouri Synod. This body had been organized in 1847. It brought a strong confessional position to American Lutheranism. It was this wing of Lutheranism in America, led by Dr. C. F. W. Walther of Concordia Seminary in St. Louis, to which the Norwegian Synod pastors felt especially drawn.

The circumstance which brought the Norwegian Synod into contact with the Missouri Synod was the need to provide a theological education for American-born and American-educated ministers. The large Norwegian immigration, and the consequent growth of congregations before the Civil War, exceeded the ability of the church to provide pastors. Despite the arrival of outstanding men (who became Synod pastors), the Synod lacked the clergy manpower to meet the spiritual needs of the frontier.

Facing the problem in 1855, at the Synod's second general convention, the Synod acted to send Pastors Brandt and Ottesen on a journey to investigate Lutheran schools at St. Louis, Columbus, and Buffalo.

Brandt and Ottesen returned with a glowing and enthusiastic recommendation that a Synod professorship be established at Concordia College and Seminary in St. Louis. They made this recommendation to the Synod's third general convention in 1857. They reported:

> How unspeakably precious it was for us to find such a beloved and richly blessed nursery for our dear Lutheran Church. . . . We noted throughout how the professors made the old Lutheran theology the basis for instruction. The symbols [i.e. the Lutheran confessional documents] were the basis for the entire instruction in dogmatics, side by side with several of the works of the best known older dogmaticians [i.e. the seventeenth century Lutheran theologians].

The committee also included, without synodical authorization, a visit to the Missouri Synod's "practical" seminary at Fort Wayne, Indiana. Here they had an equally favorable impression.

Regarding the other schools visited, Brandt and Ottesen were less enthusiastic. Confessional Lutheranism was "advancing" at Columbus, but there remained an element of instability within the Joint Synod of Ohio, which was reflected at Capital University. (It should be remembered that in 1852, when the Synod was in the process of organizing, the Synod had turned down an invitation from Capital University. One of the reasons had been the unstable confessional position at Capital and in the Joint Synod of Ohio.) Brandt and Ottesen did not recommend Capital in their report of 1857.

The Martin Luther College at Buffalo, New York, was generally quite confessional. But the Buffalo Synod, under the leadership of Pastor J. A. A. Grabau, was still espousing a hierarchical concept of the church and the ministry which was unacceptable to the Synod representatives.

The church council, upon motion by H. A. Preus, recommended to the Synod the use of Concordia College and Seminary and that a Norwegian professorship be set up there.

Meanwhile a fund would be gathered for the eventual establishment of a Synod-owned and Synod-operated educational institution, to which the Concordia professorship would then be transferred. This effort would be called "the university fund."

All this met with general approval at the Synod's 1857 general convention. Missouri's confessional theology overrode all other considerations. And soon Synod students were enrolled at St. Louis. There was some delay in obtaining a Norwegian professor for the chair at Concordia, but in 1859 Pastor Laur. Larsen accepted the call and began his teaching duties.

This was the beginning of a long-term association of the Norwegian Synod with the Missouri Synod. This association would have many satisfactory results and some strong challenges, which would last throughout the Synod's history.

## Early Doctrinal Clarifications (1853-1872)

The Synod from its beginning became defined by its stands on theological and doctrinal issues, rather than on practical and ecclesiastical programs. In most cases this stance differentiated the Synod from other Norwegian Lutheran church bodies and individuals. In a few instances it united the Synod with others.

Early in its history, in the first two decades (1853-1872) the Synod took pains to face at least five such theological issues. It was able to form and articulate a definite position on all five—presented here not necessarily in chronological order. In virtually all cases the Synod followed the Lutheran Confessions closely and issued a basic Lutheran confessional stance.

A major part of each general convention usually was devoted to a theological presentation, followed by open convention discussion of that presentation. In many cases it would reach a definite conclusion and an official position on the part of the church body.

*The first issue was the definition of the church on the basis of Scripture and the Creeds.*

The Synod opted for the precise definition of "one universal Christian church." It shied away from the definite article, "the" (or *"den"* in Norwegian) on the simple grounds that the church was not an object of faith. Instead it opted for the adjectives "one" (or the pronoun *"en"* in Norwegian) and "universal" (as a synonym for "catholic").

This stance put the Synod at odds with many low-church Norwegian Lutheran orthodox pietists, who viewed the church as "that great mass" of unbelievers as well as believers and not necessarily the church proper or the body of Christ. The Synod maintained a stronger view of the church than most Norwegian-American Lutherans.

*The second clarification was in regard to "lay activity."*

"Lay activity" was an issue in that the great Norwegian immigration to America had taken place in the wake of the Haugean awakening and revival in Norway. Most immigrants (including most pastors and members) had been influenced to some extent by the lay evangelist Hans Nielsen Hauge, who had sponsored lay activity in the Church of Norway. Thus many Norwegian Lutherans had been exposed to—or were accepting of—public prayer, teaching, and even preaching in the hands of lay members.

The Synod largely rejected "lay activity" on the basis of the Augsburg Confession, Article XIV, which reads: "It is taught among us that nobody should publicly teach or preach or administer the sacraments without a regular call."

Hence the Synod consciously and precisely invested the public ministry of the church in the ordained clergy. The only exception was the "emergency principle." The Synod early and throughout its history gave significant status always to the clergy. This position would lead to endless discussions and differences with other Norwegian Lutherans throughout the nineteenth century. A final settlement with fellow Norwegian Lutherans would be reached in the twentieth century, just prior to the Grand Union of 1917.

*The third clarification was the "Sunday question."*

Again, the immediate Haugean and pietistic background of the Norwegian Lutheran immigrants had sponsored (for many) the widespread belief that Sunday was the "Christian Sabbath." The Danish-Norwegian Explanation of Luther's Small Catechism, with which all the Norwegian immigrants were familiar, had even stated as much in dealing with the Third Commandment. Early Synod leaders, including Clausen and A. C. Preus, had maintained this position.

On closer examination, the Augsburg Confession in Article XXVIII states that "Scripture has abrogated the Sabbath Day." Luther's Large Catechism also repeats this position.

It took two general Synod conventions (1862 and 1863) to establish this confessional position for the Synod. It was apparently a new or advanced teaching for most Norwegian-American Lutherans. The theological reasoning—on the basis of Scripture—was that Christ had fulfilled (and thus Scripture had abrogated) all of the Old Testament ceremonial, civil, and moral laws. But the New Testament re-stated and re-instituted the moral law—all the commandments except the third.

The Lutheran position is that the use of God's Word makes each and every day "the Lord's Day," a stronger position than reference to one single day. This confessional position placed the Synod at odds with many of their Norwegian-American Lutheran counterparts.

*The fourth item, the doctrine of absolution, was clarified at the 1861 general convention of the Synod at Rock Prairie (Luther Valley).*

Professor Laur. Larsen presented eight theses from the Missouri Synod. Pastor B. J. Muus led the convention discussion and took issue with the basic premise in ways that would be repeated by the "orthodox pietists." The Synod theses adopted by the convention would state the "essence" rather than the "effect" of absolution. The emphasis was on the action of God, rather than the repentance and faith of the individual believer. One key controversial statement in the adopted theses was that absolution is a "powerful impartation of the forgiveness of sins."

Later—after much official discussion—all Norwegian-American Lutheran groups would in the twentieth century accept this basic position.

*Fifth, the doctrine of justification was clarified by the Synod early in its history.*

One phrase the Synod employed (from the Missouri Synod) was "justification of the world." The modern phrase is "objective and universal justification." The Synod maintained strongly that atonement from Christ alone—without faith—is the basis for forgiveness. Some other Norwegian-American Lutherans emphasized the subjective need for faith.

The Synod requested the constituting convention of the Synodical Conference in 1872 to discuss justification. The twelve theses adopted by the Synodical Conference were translated and published for Norwegian readers in a pamphlet entitled Tract No. 4.

In later official conference discussions with other Norwegian-American Lutherans, the Synod agreed to drop the phrase "justification of the world" to avoid misunderstandings. It was a phrase easily misunderstood by those who did not hold to it.

CHAPTER THREE

# Founding Pastors of the Synod

Pastors trained at the University of Oslo (Christiania) who anticipated or actually founded the Synod are as follows (including the year of arrival and the pastor's age at the time of his arrival):

J. W. C. Dietrichson, arriving in 1844, age 29

H. A. Stub, arriving in 1848, age 26

A. C. Preus, arriving in 1850, age 36

H. A. Preus, arriving in 1851, age 26

N. O. Brandt, arriving in 1851, age 27

G. F. Dietrichson, arriving in 1851, age 38

J. A. Ottesen, arriving in 1852, age 27

U. V. Koren, arriving in 1853, age 27

Laur. Larsen, arriving in 1857, age 24

B. J. Muus, arriving in 1857, age 27

The pastor who preceded all of these men, Claus L. Clausen, arriving in 1843, at age 23, was not university-educated, was Danish by background, and was ordained in America the first year he was here. Clausen was one of seven pastors on the clergy roster at the Synod's founding.

## Early Primary Leaders in the Synod

Historians point out five primary early leaders of the Synod, who served long-term, and who shaped in major ways the policies and character of the Synod. Most lived into the twentieth century. They were (including the year they passed away):

H. A. Preus (died 1894)

N. O. Brandt (died 1921)

J. A. Ottesen (died 1904)

U. V. Koren (died 1910)

Laur. Larsen (died 1915)

## Herman Amberg Preus

Preus might be called the patriarch of the Synod. He served as its president for thirty-two years (1862-1894). His position among Norwegian-American Lutherans was comparable to H. M. Muhlenberg among the East Coast Lutherans and C. F. W. Walther of the Missouri Synod.

Herman Amberg Preus

Preus' entire ministry was served at Spring Prairie (1851-1894) and surrounding congregations for forty-three years. A strong leader, he considered himself (and was) the *pater familias* of the entire Synod. The conventional wisdom was that no one dared to cross him in either the Synod or his parish. His parishioners referred to the crossroad of his church building as "the pope's corners." Preus was also a fine pastor, honored by his parishioners and their descendants for several generations. He was also an able and untiring home missionary and founder of many congregations.

As a newcomer, Preus was the driving force in the re-organization of the Synod in 1852-53 (from its "false start" in 1851) along strong confessional lines. He was reputed to be confessionally "orthodox to his finger-tips." Preus also served one term (1876-77) as president of the Synodical Conference.

## Nils Olsen Brandt

Brandt had the greatest longevity of the pioneer pastors, living to age 97. Koren, Larsen, and Stub also became octogenarians. Almost all of the Synod's first-decade pastors completed more than forty years of ordained pastoral service.

Nils O. Brandt

Brandt served at Rock River and Pine Lake in eastern Wisconsin for sixteen years. He then served a parish of three congregations (Decorah, Madison, and Lincoln) and taught at Luther College—all at Decorah, Iowa—for the remainder of his ministry. His parsonage was on the Luther campus (Campus House). He was vice president of the Synod from 1857 to 1871.

Brandt was the fifth professor named at Luther College. During his long tenure as professor and campus pastor he taught more than 900 students. Of these, 187 became pastors in the Synod. His influence, counsel, and hospitality among the students was extensive. He and his wife, Diderikke, extended themselves continuously for the student body. One Luther women's dormitory is named in her honor.

## *Jacob Aal Ottesen*

Ottesen came from a family of pastors in Norway; his family tree had no less than forty of them. He was a classmate and friend of Nils Brandt at the University of Oslo (Christiania) and had an unusually high academic record.

**Jacob Aal Ottesen**

Nonetheless, he responded to the great need for pastors in the Norwegian settlements of America's Midwest. In 1852 he became the missionary pastor of the settlements around Manitowoc, Wisconsin. In 1860 he was called to serve the Koshkonong parish and remained there thirty-one years. Ottesen was content to be the prototype of the Lutheran country pastor.

Throughout all of his ministry he served on one or more of the synodical boards. He was on the official Synod committee of two (with Brandt) sent to explore seminaries for temporary Synod use; they enthusiastically recommended Concordia at St. Louis.

But Ottesen declined official leadership positions and responsibilities within the Synod. The basic reason was that he felt inadequate. He declined the office of seminary president when the Synod founded its own seminary in 1876. He also declined the office of president of the Synod's Eastern District. He did help edit the Synod's official periodical for nine years. During Luther College's first year in Decorah (1862-63) Ottesen's parish supplied almost 50 percent of the student body.

Ottesen was described as "a power felt rather than seen." His avoidance of high-profile positions made him less a target of criticism than some of his colleagues. Yet he was a friend, counselor, and supporter of all of them. No higher compliment can be paid a man than that his friends name their sons after him. No less than six of his colleagues named their sons Jacob Aal Ottesen.

## *Ulrik Vilhelm Koren*

Koren was the pre-eminent theologian of the Synod. He was also its main dialectician and polemicist and (at times) diplomat. He was the primary scholar of the group; the others in this core group of five readily followed his theological leadership. He was the Synod's point man and spokesman in the high-profile Election Controversy.

Koren was the first pioneer Norwegian Lutheran pastor to settle west of the Mississippi River. He served the Little Iowa Parish, which surrounded Decorah and was centered at Washington Prairie (six miles southwest of Decorah) for fifty-seven years.

**Ulrich Vilhelm Koren**

It was Koren who personally procured the campus of thirty-two acres for Luther College in Decorah, and he persuaded the Synod to approve this location for their school.

He held several offices in the Synod: secretary, Iowa District president, vice president, and eventually president (1894-1910).

Koren was awarded the honorary degree Doctor of Divinity (D.D.) by Concordia Theological Seminary in 1903 at the Synod's golden anniversary.

### *Peter Laurentius (Laur.) Larsen*

Laur. Larsen was the "pack horse and work horse" of the Synod. He was also called "the Nestor of Norwegian-American schoolmen." Larsen was the first president of Luther College, serving for forty-one years in that capacity (1861-1902), more than twice the tenure of any successor. He remains the pre-eminent person in that institution's history. A distinguished alumnus has stated: "More than any other man, he has given Luther College its spirit and its traditions."

**Laur. Larsen**

Larsen was also the longtime editor-in-chief of the Synod's official periodical. In this capacity he served for a total of forty-four years, continuing for ten years after retiring from the presidency of the college, until 1912. He served as vice president of the Synod and president of the Synodical Conference.

In his very senior years Larsen became a champion and promoter of merger with the other Norwegian-American Lutheran church bodies.

Larsen was awarded an honorary degree Doctor of Divinity (D.D.) in 1903 at the Synod's golden anniversary by Concordia Theological Seminary. He was also knighted by Norway's King Haakon VII in 1908.

## Other Leaders

In addition to the founding pastors, Honorable Mention needs to be paid to at least seven other Synod leaders, all of them pastors:

### Bernt J. Muus

The founder of St. Olaf College and the first president of the Synod's Minnesota District, Muus was the perpetual gadfly who questioned virtually all of the Synod's theological positions. He was the main instigator throughout the entire Election Controversy. Muus remained faithful to the Synod, until he was removed from Synod membership. He epitomized the "loyal opposition" within the Synod.

**Bernt J. Muus**

### Evan J. Homme

Homme was the Synod's pioneer leader in charities and social services. From his base as parish pastor at Wittenberg, Wisconsin, Homme was the first to develop special care for the aged, the orphans, and the Native Americans (at that time called American Indians). In addition, he briefly operated an academy and a normal school. His actions resonate to the present day. Homme did leave the Synod during the Election Controversy, to join the Anti-Missourian Brotherhood and eventually the United Church.

### P. A. Rasmussen

The Synod's towering special pioneer in promoting support of foreign missions and the budding union movement, Rasmussen was a giant figure within the Synod, and totally loyal until the Election Controversy. He, too, joined the Anti-Missourian Brotherhood and eventually the United Church.

**P. A. Rasmussen**

### Hans G. Stub

A long-time theological professor at the Synod's Luther Seminary, Stub simultaneously served as Synod president during its last seven years (1910-1917). He became a strong promoter of church unity and guided the Synod into the Grand Union of 1917. Stub was elected the first General President of the newly-merged NLCA in 1917, and he served in that

**Hans G. Stub**

Founding Pastors of the Synod | 29

position for eight years. Stub was awarded the honorary degree, Doctor of Divinity (D.D.), by Concordia Seminary in 1903. He was knighted by Norway's King Haakon VII in 1908.

*Christian Keyser Preus*

Son of H. A. Preus, C. K. Preus was the second president of Luther College, succeeding Laur. Larsen, and serving for nineteen years (1902-1921). He also served as vice president of the Synod during its last six years (1911-1917). Preus was a leader of the Synod's minority (which sought to maintain the Synod's main-line theological position) approaching the Grand Union in 1917.

C. K. Preus

*Isaac B. Torrison*

Son-in-law of U. V. Koren, Torrison served twenty-eight years (1901-1929) as pastor of First Lutheran Church in Decorah, Iowa, the Synod's "mother congregation." He, too, was a leader of the Synod's minority in the run-up to the Grand Union of 1917.

Isaac B. Torrison

*Johannes Ylvisaker*

Ylviskaer served for thirty-eight years as theological professor at the Synod's Luther Seminary and into the NLCA's Luther Theological Seminary. He was the highly-respected chairman of the New Testament Department, and authored a valued and well-used commentary on the Gospels. Ylvisaker received the honorary degree, Doctor of Divinity (D.D.), from Concordia Seminary in 1904.

Johannes Ylvisaker

## The Office of Synod President

The presidents of the Norwegian Synod throughout its history were as follows:

    1) A. C. Preus (1853-1862)

    2) H. A. Preus (1862-1894)

    3) U. V. Koren (1894-1910)

    4) H. G. Stub (1910-1917)

CHAPTER FOUR

# The Polity of the Synod Revised

The polity of the Synod, expressed in the constitution of 1853, was soon subjected to examination and scrutiny. It was discovered to be in need of refinement, and even correction, in several areas. The Synod very soon found methods to update and correct itself.

The constitution had followed the format of the one proposed by Dietrichson in 1849. Now the Synod had been exposed to the Missouri Synod, which proved to be a corrective influence. Moreover, the orientation of the Synod had been leadership by the aristocracy; this orientation leant itself to a hierarchical structure—following the Church of Norway—and this needed to be modified.

Consequently a thorough revision was undertaken. The revised constitution was adopted in its final form in 1868, fifteen years after the first. This became the Synod's second constitution.

Among the items changed was the name. The original name—a very fine name—adopted in 1851 (and ratified in 1853) was "The Norwegian Evangelical Lutheran Church in America." The original name apparently did not "catch on" with the lay people; the membership simply referred to the church body as the "Norwegian Synod" or merely "The Synod." In recognition of this, the revised constitution altered the name to "The Synod for the Norwegian Evangelical Lutheran Church." Once again, the laity prevailed.

Another important matter which received greater emphasis in this revision was the place of the congregation in relation to the Synod. For example, the 1853 constitution vested church discipline in the synod or the church council of the synod. This was recognized as early as 1859 to be contrary to Matthew 18:17. With this new constitution it was excised. Moreover, by giving supreme authority to the Synod, congregational autonomy was seen to be endangered. The result was that henceforth the Synod was to be only advisory in respect to the congregation.

In this change the influence of the Missouri Synod was evident. Walther's controversy with Grabau (of the Buffalo Synod) on the doctrine of the church had been finalized in Walther's strong emphasis on congregational polity.

Over against Missouri, the Synod recognized itself as something less than congregational. And so the Synod moved to modify its "synodical-presbyterial" polity to a "congregational-synodical" form. This would endure throughout the Synod's history. (It would also continue beyond Synod history into the Grand Union of 1917.)

According to the new constitution, the Synod was to consist of those congregations which adopted the Synod's constitution. Voting members at synod conventions were to be lay and clergy delegates from congregations. Pastors not serving congregations were not eligible to vote, but they might qualify as "advisory" members of the convention. (This rule for convention involvement also would continue beyond Synod history into the Grand Union of 1917.)

Officers of the Synod were president, secretary, and treasurer, plus a church council composed of three pastors and three laymen; the president was the ex-officio one of the council's clergy members and president of the council.

The duties of the council were (1) to carry out the decisions of the synod, (2) to act for the synod between synod conventions, (3) to supervise the educational institutions of the Synod, (4) to examine ministerial candidates, (5) to mediate disputes upon request, (6) to exercise church discipline between synodical meetings/conventions, and (7) to supervise the Synod's finances.

The constitution of 1876 superseded the first two. It's primary concern was creating districts within the Synod, Districts were administrative units entrusted with such duties as church discipline and the reception into the Synod of those pastors and congregations within district geographical boundaries. A decision reached individually by all the districts had the same force as one reached at a general synodical convention. The entire synod itself was to meet triennially with the districts meeting separately each of the two intervening years.

The general convention of the Synod in 1876 put the new constitution into effect and then voted to create three districts:

1) Wisconsin or Eastern District. This district consisted of everything east of the Mississippi and St. Croix Rivers.

2) Iowa or Western District. This district's boundaries were west of the Mississippi River and south of a line drawn above the southern row of counties in Minnesota and extending indefinitely westward.

3) Minnesota District. This district covered the remainder of the state of Minnesota extending indefinitely westward.

District presidents chosen in 1876 were:

1) Pastor P. A. Rasmussen in the Eastern District. Rasmussen did not accept this position, however. Vice President J. B. Frich of LaCrosse served until the next district convention, when he was elected district president.

2) Pastor U. V. Koren in the Iowa District.

3) Pastor B. J. Muus in the Minnesota District.

In 1893, seventeen years later, a fourth district was added, the Pacific District. In 1908—thirty-two years later—a fifth district was formed, the Northwestern District. This district comprised North Dakota, Montana, and Canada.

CHAPTER FIVE

# Membership in the Synodical Conference

Consistent with its policy of fellowship and associations with confessionally conservative Lutherans in America, the Synod accepted the invitation from the Joint Synod of Ohio to participate with representatives of the Missouri and Wisconsin Synods in a meeting at Chicago on January 11, 1871. The purpose of this meeting was to explore the possibility of forming a federation of synods. The proposed constitution for a new "Synodical Conference" was accepted by the Synod in 1872.

The constitutional aims of the Synodical Conference were: (1) to express the existing spiritual unity, (2) to strengthen one another in faith, (3) to further unity in doctrine and in practice, and (4) to cooperate in common tasks.

As it accepted the constitution and membership, the Synod requested its delegates to bring the doctrine of justification before the Conference for discussion. The reason for this request was that many of the Synod's counterparts and opponents within Norwegian Lutheranism had charged the Synod with error in teaching "the justification of the world." The modern phrase would be "universal and objective justification."

The organizational meeting of the Synodical Conference was held in Milwaukee in 1872. It gladly discussed the Synod's propositions on justification. The Synod presentation was made by Professor F. A. Schmidt, who was leaving the Luther College faculty to take up responsibilities at Concordia Seminary as the Synod's professor. A Norwegian translation of Schmidt's theses was published under the title *Tract No. 4,* and it was enthusiastically commended to Norwegian readers.

The Synod held membership in the Synodical Conference for eleven years (1872-1883). President H. A. Preus and Professor Laur. Larsen each served one-year terms as president of the Conference. The Synod withdrew in 1883 only in the hope that this action would restore its own internal peace, which had been disrupted by the Election Controversy. The 1883 withdrawal action indicates that the desire to keep peace with fellow Norwegian-American Lutherans was stronger than the desire to associate with other confessional conservatives across nationalistic boundaries. Once again, the Synod strongly aspired for church unity.

During the eleven years of friendly association in the Synodical Conference, the Synod discovered that the strong forces of language and nationality were frequently present. These forces held Synod people back from unreserved affiliation with their German-American Lutheran friends and colleagues.

Between 1876 and 1878 the Synod considered whether to cooperate in the establishment of a joint theological seminary for the Synodical Conference. When this proposal was defeated within the Synod, the most telling arguments were appeals to nationality. Largely on the basis of this action, the Synod developed its own theological seminary—Luther Seminary at Madison, Wisconsin. A "practical" seminary department was established in 1876. The "theoretical" seminary department was moved from Concordia in St. Louis to the Madison seminary in 1878.

Through the years and until recently, the ELCA's Luther Seminary in St. Paul, Minnesota, dated its founding from the founding of the Synod's Luther Seminary in 1876. In more recent years, Luther Seminary has dated its beginning in 1869, the year that Augsburg Seminary was founded. Augsburg Seminary was merged with Luther Theological Seminary in 1963.

CHAPTER SIX

# The Slavery Issue

The first major controversy to engage the Synod internally was the Slavery Issue, which continued during a major part of the 1860s.

In 1851, when Pastors Clausen, Stub, and A.C. Preus first attempted to organize the Synod, they also began to publish *Maanedstidende* (*Monthly News*). In this publication they included strong anti-slavery articles—together with regular church news. Translation of addresses by prominent American Abolitionist leaders and others contributed to the anti-slavery views of the Synod's pioneer church members.

When Laur. Larsen—on call from the Synod—went to Concordia College and Seminary at St. Louis in 1859, he became closely associated with Professor C.F.W. Walther and other professors of the Missouri Synod. Among the views held by the highly-respected Walther was the southern theological defense of slavery on theological grounds. Early on, Walther had dissented from the viewpoint that declared slavery a sin. Walther's position was that slavery as an institution was an intermediate reality, in itself neither evil nor good; and that its use by society, as in biblical times, did not make it sinful. He admitted the abuses in slavery and urged: "Fight against the abuse, not the use." Of the abuses he said, "They [the abuses]—but not slavery itself—have cried aloud to Heaven." His arguments came to be used by the Synod pastors in the controversy that followed.

When Concordia College and Seminary suspended activities because of the Civil War and the students returned home, Larsen sent a brief notice to *Emigranten* (then the only Norwegian language newspaper in the country) about the situation. When the editor printed it, he asked Larsen for a statement of the position taken by the faculty of Concordia toward the "Rebellion"—the secession of the Confederacy and its war with the Union.

The editor went on to say that members of the Synod had shown great confidence in the Missouri institution by sending their future spiritual leaders there for training. And, he stated, that confidence would be strengthened if the faculty at Concordia were shown to be supporters of the Union instead of, like most of the Southern clergy, the Rebellion. There had been reports from some of the returning students that their teachers sympathized with the South, and this inquiry was intended to clear up the matter.

Larsen did not reply immediately. But after *Emigranten* had printed two articles from subscribers, which stirred up more comment, he answered in the June 17, 1861, issue. The editorial had inquired about the attitude of the Concordia faculty toward the Rebellion: Were they loyal to the Union? Larsen did not content himself with a simple answer to the question. He injected a defense of the view that slavery is not a sin, and referred to Roman slavery as far more cruel than American slavery. He refused to condemn secession because it was not clear that secession constituted rebellion. He also indicated that these were the views of the Concordia faculty as well as his own. But he added that, as a states' rights man, he would take up arms if ordered to do so by the governor of his state of Wisconsin.

The editor of *Emigranten* knew Larsen and was friendly toward him. He passed over the slavery issue lightly because it was not immediately relevant. He regretted that the Concordia teachers were not firmly committed to the Union. And he easily demonstrated the weakness of the states' rights position taken by Larsen. Concerning the latter, he raised the question: If Larsen were living in a slave state, would he (at the governor's call) be duty bound to fight for the South? The editor clearly did not think Larsen would do this.

Nine days later (on June 26, 1861), the Synod convened at Luther Valley, Wisconsin, for its 1861 general convention. For more than two days, the convention listened to a discussion of the doctrine of absolution lead by Laur. Larsen. But the question raised by the war—whether the Synod should continue its affiliation with Concordia, or rather establish its own college at once—was the vital one. It was tied in closely with the overriding issues of slavery and secession, which loomed large in the minds of all.

A minority group of pastors urged that the connection with St. Louis be continued until the new institution could be established. There were immediate objections—mostly from lay delegates—because of the disturbing reports about the views of the Concordia faculty. The issue became increasingly clear that slavery was tied to this issue. The convention therefore proceeded to discuss slavery. It is important to emphasize that the context of this convention discussion was the issue of college education—whether to continue with Concordia or to proceed immediately with the Synod's own institution.

Larsen—whose statement in *Emigranten* had aroused opposition—and several (but not all) of the pastors defended the viewpoint of Walther and the Missourians as to what the Bible teaches concerning slavery. Major opposition to that viewpoint was registered by the lay delegates at the convention.

The Synod leaders were in a difficult position. They knew the strong feelings of the laity. Feeling bound by the principle of separation of church and state, they hesitated to make a pronouncement on what many regarded as a political issue. They were also bound by their strict adherence to scriptural authority and were unable to refute the logic of the Southern theological interpretation of slavery.

The low-church Eielsen and Augustana Norwegian-American Lutheran synods had early taken the stand that slavery was sinful; they were therefore sympathetic to the abolitionists. But the Synod leaders were skeptical of the methods of the Abolitionist program. It was no secret, however, that the pastors (like the laymen) were opposed to American slave holding. All but one of the pastors were Republican. The deciding factor, however, was the theological one. Reflecting Scripture, what should be the Church's pronouncement on slavery?

In an effort to satisfy all parties, the pastors drew up the following resolution:

> Although, according to God's Word, it is not in and of itself sin to keep slaves, nevertheless slavery itself is an evil and a punishment from God, and we condemn all the abuses and sins connected therewith; furthermore, when our official duties require it and when Christian love and wisdom demand it, we will work for its abolition.

All the clergymen present signed the statement. When the lay delegates were asked whether they were "satisfied with this declaration as a statement of the clergymen's doctrine," they voted as follows:

Twenty-eight voted yes.

Ten voted no.

Twenty-eight did not vote.

Two were absent.

Three lay delegates who voted yes later stated they would have voted negatively had the motion been directly on slavery.

The vote on the Pastors' Declaration came as a shock to the clergy. For the first time in the history of this young Synod, they had failed to carry the laity with them. To the laity, the declaration seemed to run counter to the fundamental ideals of Norwegian immigrants. The lay members could not reconcile this pronouncement with what they knew to be the anti-slavery view of the pastors, and a majority refused to endorse it.

Nine lay members of the convention drafted the following counter-statement, which was included in the minutes of the convention:

> Slavery, viewed as an institution, can exist only under definite law, and since the laws upon which it is based stand in manifest conflict with the Word of God and Christian love, it is sin; and since slavery in the United States has been one of this country's greatest evils both for church and state, we look upon it as our absolute duty as Christians and good citizens to do everything in our power, by legal means, to alleviate, lessen, and if possible, abolish slavery, when our country's welfare and Christian love demand this of us.

This was a strong anti-slavery resolution.

Then, leaving the abstract question for the practical one before them, the convention wasted no time in getting to the school question. They decided to keep their sons up north and to proceed at once to authorize the establishment of Luther College.

As to the college's exact form and course of study, the laity did not feel competent to judge. So they left the details and the administration of the new college to Professor Laur. Larsen and the clergy. They still trusted the clergy despite the searching questions raised by the Pastors' Declaration in a time of war. The laity were so far from fanaticized that they retained Larsen in his position and placed him in charge of the institution which was now to take form up North. The Synod's laity did dictate, however, that the Synod's school, Luther College, be established on an emergency basis (within three months in 1861), well ahead of the anticipated schedule, at the beginning of the Civil War.

But the slavery matter did not end so easily. The Pastors' Declaration really rankled. Before long, Pastor C.L. Clausen, the warm-hearted Dane who for many years had cast his lot with the Norwegians, now felt constrained to withdraw his assent to the Declaration. His action was a bombshell; it made the slavery controversy inevitable. It flared up in the press in 1862; was kept in the background from 1863 to 1865; then, after the war was over, was bitterly fought from 1866 to 1869.

At first there was a gentlemen's agreement to keep the controversy out of the public eye. Clausen became the chaplain for the 15th Wisconsin Regiment and therefore was away. Clausen persuaded the Synod to refrain from public discussion until the war was over. Subduing the controversy was possible for a time.

Meanwhile, in 1862 the Synod leaders appealed to the theological faculty at the University of Christiania (Oslo) for an opinion. When it came, it offered an escape from the dilemma in which the pastors found themselves. The faculty opinion was a carefully worded document prepared by the Synod pastors' professors. It condemned slavery emphatically as contrary to God's original will for man and as a result of sin. But it acknowledged that being a slave or holding slaves is not in every instance a sin. And the New Testament nowhere expressly forbids slavery.

But the Synod leaders now took issue with their distinguished teachers. They carried on long and fruitless negotiations, hoping to persuade the university theologians to change their minds. In the formulation of the Synod rejoinders, Larsen, in particular, took a prominent part. Larsen seemed to have been the point man for the Synod on the slavery issue.

Clausen returned from the war because of ill health. Synod leaders held many conferences with him hoping to change his mind. Meanwhile, they withheld from Clausen the knowledge of the Christiania faculty documents until they were finally published in 1866, after the war was over. After the war, Clausen suggested the issue be dropped. But President H.A. Preus insisted that the authority of Scripture was the issue, and urged that the slavery question be dealt with conclusively.

After the slavery discussion had been resumed in 1866, both President H.A. Preus and Pastor Clausen made trips to Norway. Preus was on a year-long sabbatical. In 1867 both Preus and Clausen were able to spend an evening with highly-respected Professor Gisle Johnson in discussion of this issue. The results of the discussion were inconclusive. Each man thought Johnson had sided with him. But Professor Johnson did make one sagacious comment that evening; namely, that this was an issue to be decided by history rather than by the Scriptures and theology.

When discussion resumed back home, Clausen was no match for the dialecticians arrayed against him—Larsen, Schmidt, Ottesen, H.A. Preus, and Koren—not to mention several Missourians who were brought in to bolster Synod pastors. In the heat of debate, Clausen became involved in contradictions that weakened his case. The Synod leaders were therefore able to discredit him. At the 1868 general convention, they carried the day by an overwhelming majority. They did so in the name of preserving "the pure doctrine." The Pastors' Resolution of 1861 passed and became the official policy of the Synod.

It was a Pyrrhic victory. In 1869, the Synod again took up the subject. They did so perhaps as a result of Pastor A.C. Preus' "Word of Reconciliation," in which he defended the Christiania faculty opinion. This time the Synod declared that American slavery "in the less precise speech of daily life" was a sin. The Synod also maintained that masters who treated their slaves "in love according to God's Word" did not sin by keeping slaves. The church council then proceeded to say, "No Christian can be a pro-slavery man." Thus the Synod finally declared slavery a sin in 1869.

Laur. Larsen's daughter, Professor Karen Larsen, writes: "Had there been no connection with the Missouri Synod, the issue of slavery might never have been raised. . . . To uphold the authority of Scriptures was a *sine qua non* to the clergy. Unless they should change their whole method of biblical interpretation, they had to maintain that slavery was not a sin."

The Synod men argued from the premise that the words of the Scriptures, inerrant because verbally inspired, were logically identified with the Word of God. Walther confirmed and encouraged them in their position. They persuaded themselves, Walther and Synod leaders alike, that they were upholding the sacredness of Scripture against the mistaken notions of less enlightened men.

Walther did not guide the Synod leaders to a more conciliatory attitude and an abandonment of their early positions; on the contrary, he urged them not to yield an inch. At the same time, he did not permit the slavery issue to come up for discussion in his Missouri Synod. Walther was probably not the right mentor to the Synod clergy on this particular issue. He did not really understand the Norwegian mentality. He was one or two steps removed from the actual Norwegian Synod situation, never an actual part of it. Larsen, during his senior years, admitted that his youth and the youth of his colleagues contributed to the controversy.

There was fallout. In 1868, at the height of the discussion, Clausen was denied Holy Communion because he went contrary to the Synod position. They placed him under church discipline and denied him admission to the Lord's Table. He resigned from the Synod immediately after the 1868 general convention. He affiliated with other Norwegian-American Lutheran groups, becoming president of the Norwegian-Danish Conference. Pastor A.C. Preus acted four years later, in 1872. He returned to Norway to serve the remainder of his ministry in the state church. He cited the slavery controversy as the reason.

## Observations

The slavery issue was the first major controversy in the Norwegian Synod. It came during the first quarter century of its life. It is important to note ten observations on the slavery controversy:

There was no agreement on the issues. This can always lead to a red-hot controversy. Resolutions can come only when the issues are engaged. The clergy regarded the Authority of Scripture as the primary issue. They were regularly confronted with the cults, sects, aberrations, and general chaos of the frontier. This was their day-to-day challenge. The laity regarded the real issue as the practical, down-to-earth reality of the monstrous evil of slavery. Along with this, they were engrossed in the preservation of the Union and the reality that their sons were fighting and dying for the cause.

The laity (as usual) had the last word. Luther College was established on an emergency basis. And, in 1869, the slavery issue was put to rest and never raised again.

The Missouri Synod was not a good mentor on this issue. Missouri's role created widespread suspicion which would aggravate the Election Controversy two decades later. The University of Christiania, Norway, professors were excellent mentors. They were the distinguished teachers of most of the clergy. Their proposed solution was by far the most viable.

The youth and immaturity of the Synod leaders were apparent at this early point in the Synod's history. Some of those leaders later, in their senior years, admitted this.

The clergy could have/should have been more pastoral. The pastors needed to observe and empathize with the laity's viewpoint, or put themselves in the laity's shoes.

There was something false about this whole controversy. At no time was Synod geographical territory threatened. And the real controversy was engaged after the fact—after the Southern surrender and the abolition of slavery itself. Further, no protagonists were actual promoters of slavery. Nor were any accused of being so.

The Synod lost two distinguished pastors because of how it handled the controversy. Claus Clausen, who had been a leader in the Synod for twenty-five years, since the Muskego congregation was founded, was badly mistreated. His conscience should have been respected. He never should have been forced into open debate, for which he was not prepared. A.C. Preus had been the first Synod president, serving even before the Synod was fully organized (1852-1862). He had been on the frontier scene twenty-two years (1850-1872) before returning to serve the rest of his ministry in the state Church of Norway, primarily because of this struggle within the Synod.

Several congregations were lost to the Synod. Many returned later, but with the loss of several members.

More positively: The Synod did finally settle this issue in 1869 after the fact. Most often the Synod did settle its issues favorably. And again, the laity had the last word. They were the ones who prevailed.

CHAPTER 7

# Inter-Synodical Theological and Doctrinal Discussions

During the two decades from 1860 to 1880 the Synod was involved in a number of discussions, and even controversies, with other Norwegian Lutheran church bodies. Doctrinal dialogue was the basis of inter-synodical contact on the part of the Synod with other church groups. It seems that each body gave a high priority to doctrine, especially the Norwegian Synod. And each would require that "you must agree with me." This general and universal requirement of agreement caused difficulty with other church bodies.

During the 1860s the Synod discussed the doctrine of absolution with the Scandinavian Augustanans. And during the 1870s, the Synod discussed gospel and justification with the Norwegian-Danish Conference. It has been pointed out that the strife which resulted from these major discussions was essentially the clash of two opposing points of view: (1) The first strongly emphasized the objectivity of the truth. (2) The second embraced the Haugean and "orthodox pietist" emphasis on the personal appropriation of truth. In other words, they struggled with objective and subjective points of view. Almost always the Synod contended for the objectivity of truth, or the confessionally objective point of view.

Historians point out that the Synod, with the support of the Missouri Synod, had only systematized what most Norwegian Lutherans had believed, taught, and confessed from the earliest days. This historical insight was a real compliment to Norwegian Lutheranism in general and the Synod's doctrinal articulation in particular. But it was the demand for agreement on the part of all parties that enhanced these inter-synodical discussions into debate and even strife.

## Inter-Synodical Discussions in the 1860s

In the 1860s, the Synod and the Scandinavian Augustanans struggled to agree on specific theological points. At the outset, beginning as early as 1859, their inter-synodical conversations were convened to bring about friendly relations, and the Synod was eager to participate. However, the more they got together, the more they disagreed, and the more unhappy they both became.

In the year 1861 at the annual general convention of the Synod (at Luther Valley, the same convention which authorized the founding of Luther College) Professor Laur. Larsen presented a paper. Larsen was fresh from his experiences as a professor at Concordia Seminary. His full-dress presentation to the convention was on the doctrine of absolution. It took two days. As a basis for the discussion, Professor Larsen introduced eight theses prepared by a Missouri Synod pastor. These propositions spelled out the Missourian viewpoint, which the Synod found so congenial and would maintain in the future. Included in one of these theses was the definition of absolution as "a powerful impartation of the forgiveness of sins."

The pastor whom Larsen had persuaded to accept the call to the Holden Parish near Kenyon, Minnesota, Pastor B. J. Muus, rose to challenge his friend's use of the words, "a powerful impartation." Muus contended that the phrase implies that God gives forgiveness of sins also to unbelievers. This led to considerable discussion on the floor of the convention.

Three years later, in 1864, the Synod and the Scandinavian Augustanans met in an inter-synodical gathering at Jefferson Prairie. They found themselves facing the same questions as the Synod had at Luther Valley. The Augustanans, using Muus's objection, said the gospel "offers the forgiveness of sins to all who hear it; but this forgiveness is given, imparted, and presented only to those who in faith receive it." The position of the Synod was stated as follows: "The preaching of the Gospel . . . imparts the forgiveness of sins to all to whom it is proclaimed, whether they believe it or not (although it is not accepted by all)."

The concern of the Augustanans was to uphold the place of faith. The Synod stressed the sovereignty of grace in relation to the salvation of man. This divine action is the content of the Gospel as proclaimed in the absolution; as such, it is not affected by faith or unbelief. The Synod looked at the gospel and absolution from above. The content of the gospel remains unchanged, whether one believes it or not, but it benefits no one unless one believes. The gospel is a declaration of forgiveness. The Augustanans looked at the gospel and absolution from below. They stressed the need of convincing sinners that they are sinners, thus needing repentance and faith. For them, the gospel is the offer of forgiveness.

Pastor U. V. Koren, one of the Synod's strongest theologians, possessed the keen ability to discern issues. In 1867 he tried to intervene with a "friendly word" that the disagreement centered on the "essence" of the gospel rather than its "effect." This could have, and should have, solved the controversy. But in spite of this "friendly word" from a strong theologian, agreement was not forthcoming. The conflict picked up steam, the two sides never quite meeting head-on, and was characterized by more heat than light.

Eventually there would be a reconciliation of these views and debates after the turn of the twentieth century. In 1906 all parties agreed on a statement covering the doctrine of absolution. Finally, this issue was settled.

## Inter-Synodical Discussions in the 1870s

The year 1870 saw the Scandinavian Augustana Synod re-organized into two bodies: The Norwegian Augustana Synod, and the Norwegian Danish Conference. The Conference was the larger of the two bodies. Pastor C.L. Clausen, who had resigned from the Synod just two years earlier (in 1868), became president of the Conference.

It was with the Conference that the Synod would dialogue primarily in the 1870s. The Conference had largely inherited the conversation with the Synod from its predecessor. But now the issue had changed to the Doctrine of Justification.

This inter-synodical controversy lead to a few "free conferences," rather than official synodical discussions. A free conference was made up of individuals, rather than official synodical representatives.

The first of these free conferences was held in Decorah, Iowa, during June 1871. It gave the promise of better feeling between synods. And the Synod appears to have happily hosted this gathering. However, progress was derailed with the confrontation of a new antagonist; namely, the German Iowa Synod. In 1872 the Iowa Synod charged the Synod with heresy in its teaching of the "justification of the world." The result was that the Synod requested the constituting convention of the Synodical Conference (1872) in Milwaukee to discuss the doctrine of justification.

The Synodical Conference was made up of the Missouri Synod, the Wisconsin Synod, the Joint Synod of Ohio, and the Norwegian Synod. It initially was formed by synods which declined membership in the recently formed General Council (1867), which became a predecessor body of the ULCA (1918), and eventually the LCA (1962). The Synodical Conference began its long life by devoting its initial convention to what was to become its chief concern—doctrinal discussion.

The twelve theses on justification adopted at Milwaukee, and the discussion around them, were subsequently translated and published in a fifty-one page pamphlet known as *Tract No. 4*. In this pamphlet was set the orderly presentation of the Synod's position on matters around which there had been controversy, not least now on "justification of the world" (today called "universal and objective justification"). The viewpoint was basically the same as that set forth by the Synod in the absolution controversy of the 1860s. The Synodical Conference strongly supported the Synod's position on justification.

Later that same year (November 1872) another "free conference" took place at Rock Prairie (Luther Valley), Wisconsin. Using the twelve theses, of *Tract No. 4,* as the basis of discussion, the participants once again foundered on "justification of the world." The Norwegian-Danish Conference maintained that no one is justified before having faith (which seems to be implied in "justification of the world"). The Synod emphasized that the atonement of Christ alone (without faith) is the basis of forgiveness. To say that faith, as well as the atonement, is the basis for justification would mean that man contributes to his salvation. Thus the Synod shifted the discussion to the atonement as the basic issue.

It was at Rock Prairie (Luther Valley) that President H.A. Preus issued his judgment, called his "bull of excommunication," citing St. Paul's anathema in Galatians 1: 6-8. It was directed at the Conference for its "heretical position" on justification. This "bull" of 1872 has been termed the "burr" in the Conference's fur for years to come and effectively ended free conferences for a whole decade.

It was against this "bull" that two leaders of the Conference, Professors Oftedal and Weenaas of Augsburg Seminary, issued their *Public Declaration* of 1874. The *Public Declaration* was an inflammatory publication and was published in the secular newspaper *Skandinaven*. It was directed at "Wisconsinism," the popular negative description of the Synod's stated positions. The *Declaration* charged the Synod with unbalanced scholastic and intellectual orthodoxy, which produced contempt for religious awakenings. It also charged the Synod with the desire to rule the church from the top. It continued: The essence of Christianity is corrupted; the congregations' rights and the people's freedom is denied. What is this but popery? And now the Synod, through its application of scholastic orthodoxy to the life of the church is guilty of both "theoretical" and "practical" Catholicism. Dedicated to opposite principles, the *Declaration* continued, the Conference could no more be reconciled with the Synod "than Christ and Belial, fire and water." (This was strong and uncalled for language by the *Declaration*.)

The charges against the Synod were clearly of the most serious nature. But historians point out that the charges were unsupported by any proof whatsoever in the document itself. Those attacked could be hardly expected to remain silent.

"Proofs" and rebuttals were forthcoming in two pamphlets, one by Professor Weenaas (of the Conference), the other by President H.A. Preus (of the Synod). The Weenaas-Preus exchange ended two years later (1876) with Weenaas returning to Norway. In many respects, the exchange had not resolved but rather heightened the tensions between the Synod and the Conference. Perhaps it did sharpen some of the issues.

Preus appears to have answered Weenaas' charges against the Synod more than adequately. It would also seem that Weenaas' return to Norway may have resulted in part from this confrontation and exchange. The controversy did not subside with the departure of Weenaas for Norway. Two remaining leaders of the Conference—Professors Oftedal and Sverdrup (both of Augsburg Seminary)—took up the mantle, promoting the free-church movement. They also promoted and exalted Luther's Catechism and Pontoppidan's explanation of Luther's Catechism, *Truth Unto Godliness*, as being sufficient for doctrinal formulation—as over against the other Lutheran Confessions and further Lutheran theological scholarship.

The Augsburg Seminary professors, Oftedal and Sverdrup, were products of the Church Reform movement in Norway, where the issue of a free congregation and a free church was crucial and relevant. In America they were, to a large extent, indulging in destroying straw men. In America the slogan of "a free congregation in a free church" did not have the same relevance as in Norway; many Norwegian-American Lutheran people simply could not understand their dwelling on the theme of freedom. Their confronting the Synod with vivid memories of the Church of Norway and espousing "a free congregation and a free church" seemed to be mouthing an empty phrase.

From the Synod came answers to the Augsburg professors—especially from Larsen, Preus, Stub, Schmidt, and Koren. Koren, the Synod's premier theologian, for example, charged the Conference theologians with employing empty phrases, sophistry, and high-sounding terms. They were guilty of "proving" what the Synod had never denied, and "denying" what the Synod had never attempted to prove. On top of all this, the Conference which supported them was not doctrinally united. In fact, that which kept the Conference from falling apart was a common enmity toward the Synod. Thus the Synod accused the Conference of ambiguous use of words and fuzzy definition of intentions.

The issue of justification pointed forward to a quiet settlement in the Union Movement of the early twentieth century.

## Consequences of the 1870s

The consequences of the Synod-Conference conflict of the 1870s were not limited to theological discussions. It quite naturally caused damage on the local scene and the international scene.

Locally, the conflict was reflected on the parish level by fierce competition for members of rival congregations. The Synod seems to have been especially sensitive to pastoral and parish ethics. But charges and countercharges of proselytizing and of unethical transgressions of parish boundaries were sounded by both sides.

Overseas, the inter-synodical strife in America was reflected in cooling relationships between the Church of Norway and the Synod. Leaders of the Synod (in their increasing commitment to confessionalism) became more and more critical of the mother church. Weenaas, who observed this, commented that the Synod was not a true daughter of the Church of Norway, but of the German Missouri Synod.

## Effects on the Norwegian Mission Society

The controversy placed the Norwegian Mission Society in difficult position. It was an organization independent of the state church, but supported by members of the Church of Norway. Beginning in 1869-1870, the congregations of the Synod had cooperated with the Norwegian Mission Society by sending contributions to it directly or through the mission treasurer of the Synod. In fact, the Synod was granted a sort of associate membership in the society because of the interest of Synod leadership and members in foreign missions.

In 1873, the Conference petitioned and was granted the same recognition. The Synod considered this situation intolerable because it brought the Synod informally (by default) into fellowship with the Conference. Laur. Larsen wrote, "...there is no unity of faith between them (the Conference) and us. How we shall now both stand in the same relation to the Society is difficult to understand." In 1874 the Synod voted to sever relations with the Society unless it cut its ties with the Conference.

The Society, obviously reluctant to lose the support of the Conference, tried to negotiate with the Synod, while at the same time maintaining its connection with the Conference.

Because the Synod was unable to come to a satisfactory agreement with the Society, it decided to permit each congregation to determine whether or not it would support the Society. This was a benevolent and mission-minded decision.

## The Synod's Judgment of 1880

As the decade of the 1870s gave way to the 1880s, a major development took place in the Synod-Conference face-off, the Synod's 1880 "judgment" of the Conference.

In 1880 Pastor P. A. Rasmussen of the Synod sought to initiate action leading to the eventual union of all Norwegian Lutheran church bodies in America. When Rasmussen's union proposal was presented to the Minnesota District of the Synod, the assembly expressed its opinion of the Conference in such a way that it created a vast amount of resentment within the Conference. District President B.J. Muus, who was never friendly to the Conference, may have been behind this move.

A portion of an official report, adopted by a vote of thirty-four to seventeen, explicitly stated that the Kingdom of God was being furthered, not hindered, by the strife with the Conference. It further stated that the Synod had little in common with the Conference *because* the Conference had a completely different faith and confession from that found in the Word of God and the Lutheran Symbolical Books. The force of this "judgment" lay in its official character. Before this, such strong statements as Preus' "bull" and Oftedal's (with Weenaas) *Public Declaration* had been merely the pronouncement of individuals. Now a segment of the Synod had spoken officially; and its tones were negative and blunt. The "judgment" would be felt for some time.

Although the conversations between church bodies in the 1870s were warm and hopeful, the prospects for friendly inter-synodical relations in the 1880s were not very promising.

CHAPTER EIGHT

# Publications

The Synod had a major commitment to education and keeping its membership fully informed. Therefore, official and un-official publications were primary to the Synod's existence and function.

The printed word had been essential to the church ever since Johannes Gutenberg invented the printing press, just prior to the Reformation. Publications were continually significant in spreading and maintaining the Christian faith. Thus the printed word was an extremely effective part of the church's mission.

The Synod tapped right into this heritage from its beginning—and even before. Immediately from its inception, the Synod invested heavily and effectively in its publications. The printed word was part and parcel of the Synod's mission. The Synod was the first Norwegian-American Lutheran church body to publish an official periodical. And it published three successive periodicals.

The first was *Maanedstidende* (*Monthly News*), which preceded the Synod's official existence. It began January 1, 1851, and it generally co-existed with the Synod's first two-year attempt to organize (the "false start"). The founders sought to have an official publication in place at the very beginning of the church body itself. The editors were three pastors: A. C. Preus, C. L. Clausen, and H. A. Stub. Its publication would lapse two years later in 1853 at the Synod's official beginning.

The second was *Kirkelig Maanedstidende* (*Churchly Monthly News*), which began in March 1855, a year-and-a-half after *Maanedstidende* ceased publication. *Kirkelig Maanedstidende* began as a monthly, but it eventually became a bi-monthly publication. *Kirkelig Maanedstidende* would last until 1874, a total of nineteen years, when it would be replaced by a successor periodical.

*Kirkelig Maanedstidende* was edited by the pastors of the Synod. By 1860 Pastor H. A. Preus was listed as the sole editor. Within the next year Preus made it clear that the editorship was too much for him alone and requested help in sharing the responsibility. Pastor J. A. Ottesen was solicited to assist Preus, and they co-edited this publication from 1861 to 1868.

In 1868 the editorship was transferred to the faculty of Luther College, with President Laur. Larsen as editor-in-chief. The faculty edited *Kirkelig Maanedstidende* until 1874 and its successor until 1902, a total of thirty-four years.

The third Synod periodical was *Evangelisk-Luthersk Kirketidende* (*Evangelical Lutheran Church News*), which began January 2, 1874, the successor of *Kirkelig Maanedstidende*. *Evangelisk-Luthersk Kirketidende* was a weekly. It would continue for the remainder of the Synod's existence, until 1917, for a total of forty-three years. *Evangelisk-Luthersk Kirketidende* would be the best known and most influential of the three successive Synod publications.

The Luther College faculty continued to edit *Evangelisk-Luthersk Kirketidende* with President Laur. Larsen as editor-in-chief until his retirement from the college presidency in 1902. Following Larsen's retirement from the presidency he would remain as sole editor-in-chief for ten more years, until 1912. Thus Dr. Laur. Larsen would serve as editor-in-chief of *Kirkelig Maanedstidende* and then *Evangelisk-Luthersk Kirketidende* for a total of forty-four years. No wonder Larsen was called the "pack horse" and the "work horse" of the Synod.

In 1906 the Synod began its English publication, *Lutheran Herald*. The Synod was the first of the Norwegian-American Lutheran church bodies to sponsor an English-language periodical.

The editors of the *Lutheran Herald* were Pastor H. B. Hustvedt (1906-1909), Pastor (later Professor) Theodore C. Graebner of the Missouri Synod (1909-1913), and Pastor G. T. Lee (1913-1917).

The *Lutheran Herald* became the official periodical in the Grand Union (1917) of the newly-merged church body, the Norwegian Lutheran Church in America (NLCA), which became the Evangelical Lutheran Church (ELC) in 1946. Pastor Lee continued as editor-in-chief until 1939, for a total of twenty-six years. In 1939 another Synod-heritage pastor, Dr. O. G. Malmin, became the editor-in-chief and served in that capacity until 1960. The *Lutheran Herald* remained the official periodical of the NLCA/ELC throughout its entire history of forty-three years (1917-1960).

The Synod was prolific in several other publications, as well. There were seven other periodicals published within the Synod during its history:

1) *The Watchman* (1866-1867) was an English-language periodical edited by the young Professor F. A. Schmidt of Luther College.

2) *For the Home* (in translation) (1970-1888), published at Decorah, was "an entertaining and instructive monthly magazine," and was widely read.

3) *Children's Paper* (in translation) began in 1875 and was published by the Synod for the duration of its history, until 1917.

4) *Picture Magazine* (in translation), published in Madison (1868-1870), was noted for its excellent articles on pioneer settlements.

5) *Periodical for the Edification of Lutheran Christians* (in translation) was issued as a monthly (1877-1887) by distinguished Pastor P. A. Rasmussen of Lisbon, Illinois.

6) *For Old and Young* (in translation) was published by the eminent and indefatigable Pastor E. J. Homme of Wittenberg, Wisconsin, from 1881 until his death in 1903. It was an interesting collection of stories, anecdotes, mission news, church news, poems, and riddles.

7) *Theological Review* (in translation) was a later publication provided by Luther Seminary's theological faculty under the editorship of Dr. H. G. Stub. It continued for the tenure of the Synod. After the Grand Union (1917) it continued under the editorship of a Synod-heritage pastor, Dr. Rasmus Malmin.

In addition, a distinguished and long-term secular newspaper was begun by Synod people: *Emigranten* (*The Emigrant*) began publishing on January 23, 1852. *Emigranten* became the most influential of all the pioneer secular newspapers among the Norwegians in America. It was described as an Independent-Democratic publication. *Emigranten* was published by the Scandinavian Press Association, located at Luther Valley, Wisconsin, with several Synod pastors among the association incorporators: A. C. Preus, G. F. Dietrichson, and H. A. Preus. Pastor C. L. Clausen was chosen as the first editor. *Emigranten* early stimulated interest in American national politics. It carried controversial articles pertaining to political parties and personalities. It also published material which covered then-current church controversies. *Emigranten* also covered news from Norway.

Pastor Clausen remained editor for only eight months. He was succeeded by Charles M. Reese, who was succeeded by Knud J. Fleischer.

In 1857, when the paper was moved from Luther Valley (Immansville) to Madison, Carl Fredrick Solberg took over the editing. He became the greatest of *Emigranten*'s several editors. He served eleven years. Editor Solberg was also an ardent Lutheran. He was a good friend of Synod pastors. But he did raise the slavery issue within the Synod, which made it a strong controversy. Incidentally, Solberg was a strong supporter of President Abraham Lincoln. He published Lincoln's *Emancipation Proclamation* in full and in Norwegian.

In 1868 *Emigranten* was sold to a LaCrosse firm, and in 1886 it was moved to Minneapolis. In 1896 it was merged with *Minneapolis Tidende* (*Minneapolis News*), continuing until 1935, for a total of eighty-three years. In 1935 its subscription list was taken over by *Decorah Posten*.

The Synod succeeded strongly in publications, even when it ventured into secular journalism. Printer's ink played a strong and vital role in the Synod's life and history.

CHAPTER NINE

# Worship and Church Music

The original Synod forebears invariably brought four books with them in their immigration to America: the Bible, Luther's Small Catechism, a book of sermons, and the family hymnbook.

There were a number of hymnbooks from which to choose in the Norwegian-Danish tradition, and many were used in the early years of the Synod. In 1870 the Synod published its own hymnbook. There were four editors, including chiefly Pastor U. V. Koren. Koren personally contributed twenty-seven original hymns and twenty-one translations to this first hymnbook. The Synod also produced its own melody book. (Evidently early hymnals included words only.)

For the most part, these hymns were in minor keys with somber themes, which had been inherited from Norway and reflected the hardships of life in Norway and of the American frontier.

Early on there were no translations of English-language hymns into Norwegian, nor from Norwegian into English. The Synod lived with the Norwegian language for several decades.

In 1884 the first English hymnbook was published. It was a humble little handbook of 130 hymns. In 1898 a modest Sunday school hymnbook was published.

In 1898 also came the first official Synod hymnbook in English, entitled *Christian Hymns for Church, School, and Home*. It contained 309 hymns.

Synod music people were prolific. The Synod also produced a number of freelance Norwegian and English hymnbooks. Early Synod choir songbooks included *Songbook for Beginners and Young People* (1878), *Songbook for Church Choirs* (1884), *Scandinavian Songs* (1890), *Sexton-Tones* (1896), and *Songbook for Church Choirs* (1896).

After the turn of the century, the Synod produced *Choir Songs* (1903), a widely-used anthem book, and *Church Songs (Hymns) for Mixed Choirs* (1905).

President Stub's wife, Valborg Hovind Stub, who was a recognized soloist, edited *Songs from the North*, which was a major contribution to solo singing.

The Choral Union of the Synod was organized in 1903, at the Golden Jubilee of the church body. The Choral Union was the mass choir made up of delegates at Synod general and district conventions. Pastor J. W. Preus was the first president of the Choral Union (1903-1917). Jacob Hjort was the first director. Professor John Dahle of Luther Seminary was a major figure in the Choral Union, as were the Koren and Forde families, along with many others.

The tradition of the Choral Union continued and was inherited and maintained throughout the history of the Synod's successor, the NLCA. It was a real contribution to the church body's corporate life.

In 1908 the Synod took the initiative and approached the two other church bodies involved in union negotiations concerning a possible new English-language hymnal. The result was a special inter-synodical committee, authorized by the Synod, the United Church, and Hauge's Synod, to compile a common treasury of hymns and liturgical materials. Six Synod people served on this first inter-synodical committee.

The final result of five years' hard work by this special inter-synodical committee was, in 1913, *The Lutheran Hymnary*. This hymnal became the standard hymn and worship service book for almost the next half-century (for at least forty-five years, from 1913 to 1958). Someone wrote: "As a 'transition' hymnbook it has done much to maintain high standards and bridge the gap between Norwegian and English, and to preserve for posterity the heritage of our fathers."

*The Lutheran Hymnary* also gave rise to three companion popular hymnals: *The Lutheran Hymnary Junior*, the "Old" *Concordia Hymnal*, and the "New" *Concordia Hymnal*.

Great contributors to the strong Synod music program were its two foremost educational institutions, Luther Seminary and Luther College.

At Luther Seminary Professor John Dahle was the instructor in hymnody and director of the seminary choir. For many years he was the (informal) music director for the entire Synod. He edited many books for male and mixed choruses. He supplied many anthems for congregational use. Among many other contributions, he wrote a cantata for the 900th anniversary of Christianity in Norway, and another cantata for Luther College's sixtieth anniversary.

Professor Dahle aided the organization of the Synod's Choral Union and served as its director. He was also a major contributor to *The Lutheran Hymnary*. As a professor and choir director at Luther Seminary, he remained a much-loved and colorful contributor to Synod hymnody into old age.

At Luther College a long list of music instructors and musical organizers began their service when it was established (1861) and continued without interruption.

In 1905 Professor Carlo A. Sperati came to Luther and took over the music program. He made the Luther College Concert Band world famous. Sperati was identified with many branches and fields of music for the Synod, including the Choral Union. At Luther he established the tradition of Handel's "Messiah" each year, a tradition that lasted most of the twentieth century. He was the Grand Old Man of the Synod in music.

The liturgical practices of the Dano-Norwegian Church were carefully followed by the Synod. Traditional forms of worship were maintained, including the chanting of the collects (prayers), the benediction, and the communion service. Five congregational hymns were standard for Sunday worship. Worship in Synod congregations was always very formal. The old forms were maintained. The entire worship heritage was scrupulously preserved. In all forms of worship, the Synod employed and contributed greatly to church music.

The historic vestments of the Norwegian state church pastors were carefully preserved: the loose-fitting black cassock, the stole, and the white-fluted collar. (Photos show that pioneer pastor J. W. C. Dietrichson also wore a heavy chasuble.)

# CHAPTER TEN

# The Election Controversy

The Election Controversy of the 1880s was the most traumatic episode in the Synod's history. It came at the half-way point in the Synod's life. The issue developed like an explosion out of nowhere. Few saw it coming; it caught most by surprise. No rational discussion or serious conferences or well-intentioned disagreements led up to it. The controversy simply came out of the blue and mushroomed out-of-hand before it could be recognized or assessed. There was significant fall-out.

The open debate which followed all took place within the one Lutheran doctrine of election. What would emerge would be two so-called "forms" of this one unified doctrine. With their mentor, Martin Luther, both sides (first and second form) regarded election or predestination as a source of comfort for all believers, an assurance of God's saving love.

The following definition sums up the first form position: "Election is that act of God from eternity, who before the foundations of the world were laid, solely because of God's grace and mercy, and the holy merits of Christ, resolved to call, justify, and glorify those who finally would be saved." According to first form, election is unrelated to anything God might foresee in the human being, including faith.

The first form was advocated by the Missouri Synod and by many influential pastors in the Norwegian Synod; in fact, it became basically the position of the Synod. It was derived from Article XI of the Formula of Concord, one of the Lutheran Confessional documents. From the Formula of Concord, Article XI (Full Declaration) we have this explanatory statement: "The eternal election of God, however, not only foresees and foreknows the salvation of the elect, but is also from the gracious will and pleasure of God in Jesus Christ, a cause which procures, works, helps, and promotes our salvation and what pertains thereto; and upon this [divine predestination] our salvation is so founded that the gates of hell cannot prevail against it."

The second form of the Lutheran doctrine of election is based on Danish Lutheran Bishop Erik Pontoppidan's definition in his explanation of Luther's Small Catechism, entitled *Truth Unto Godliness*. This was the definition on which most Norwegian Lutherans had been raised and instructed since childhood—both laity and clergy.

Answering the question, "What is election?" the explanation answers: "God has appointed all those to eternal life who He from eternity has foreseen would accept the offered grace, believe in Christ, and remain constant in this faith unto the end."

The second form understanding originated with Professor Aegidius Hunnius, an orthodox Lutheran theologian of the sixteenth century, who taught at Marburg and Wittenberg Universities in Germany. He was known for his opposition to Calvinism. His definition of election is as follows: "Election is that act of God from eternity which before the foundation of the world was laid determined to glorify all those who He foresaw would come to faith in Christ until the end."

The difference of second form from first form is the concept that God appoints persons to salvation "in view of foreseen faith" (*intuitu fidei*). This phrase, "in view of foreseen faith," was Hunnius' contribution to the discussion. "In view of foreseen faith" would become the controversial flash-point in this internal Synod debate.

The Synod leaders taught and advocated first form. They found their leader in Pastor U. V. Koren, who more than anyone shaped their approach to the problem. Professor F. A. Schmidt and Pastor B. J. Muus along with several allies promoted second form.

The process was very confrontational. Few, if any, attempts were made to deal with the issues rationally. Genuine attempts at reconciliation were few. The whole process, sadly, was an out-of-control rush to alienation and division. It was civil war. Because confrontation and schism are always tragedies for any church body, the unresolved nature of this episode was a tragedy which should have been avoided by recognizing a number of "alerts" which could have alerted leaders to the controversy lurking below the surface.

## The Controversy Develops at the Seminary

The issue over the doctrine of election first appeared in the Synod when one of the two original professors at the Synod's new Luther Seminary in Madison took issue with Missourianism in the Synod.

Professor Ole Asperheim raised this issue at a pastoral conference in Milwaukee in February 1878. Later he published a book, entitled *The Missouri Synod and the Norwegian Synod,* in which he criticized the Missouri Synod in the most scathing terms. Charging Missouri with perverting doctrine, Asperheim singled out election as exhibit A; he charged that Missouri's teaching on election was dangerously poised between Calvinism and seventeenth century Lutheran orthodoxy. Asperheim went on to advocate that the Synod break with Missouri.

Asperheim was almost immediately *persona non grata* in the Synod. Even his one colleague on the seminary faculty, Professor F. A. Schmidt, opposed him. Asperheim soon resigned his professorship to accept a call as seaman's pastor in New York City.

Professor Schmidt, however, was soon in the center of the controversy. He took explicit issue with his former friend, Missouri Synod patriarch C. F. W. Walther. It was Walther who had recommended Schmidt to the Synod in 1861, when the Synod needed another professor (in addition to Laur. Larsen) at Luther College. Now suddenly Schmidt attacked Walther's position on election. He reported his reasons in his pamphlet, "The Election Controversy."

In that publication, Schmidt states that two weeks after Asperheim's anti-Missourian charges at Milwaukee, he read Walther's address on election delivered before the 1877 Western District convention of the Missouri Synod. Walther elaborated on Article XI of the Formula of Concord in this way: "God foresaw nothing, absolutely nothing in those whom He resolved to save which might be worthy of salvation; even if it be admitted that he saw some good in them, this nevertheless could not have determined Him to elect for that reason; for, as the Scriptures teach, all good in man originates in Him." Walther, discussing the place of faith, went on to say: "Faith, therefore, is not a condition by which God saves us. It is much rather a requisite which He Himself will supply."

Walther went on to argue that the terminology employed by some of the seventeenth century Lutheran theologians was unfortunate. Some had employed the term, *intuitu fidei* (in view of foreseen faith) which they employed not to promote synergism (working with God), but to combat Calvinism.

According to Schmidt, Walther's position smelled like Calvinistic determinism, which was to be opposed. At first Schmidt expressed his opposition by letter and conversation. But by 1879 he was convinced that a more positive protest needed to be registered. Therefore, in 1880 "in order to ring the storm bell" he began publishing the periodical *Altes und Neues* (The Old and the New [Doctrine]).

With the appearance of this periodical, the lines in the Synod were drawn. Pastor U. V. Koren, the Synod's leading theologian and the chief promoter of the Missourian position in the Synod, made the issue personal immediately by stating that any attack on Walther and the Missouri Synod was equivalent to "an attack upon himself." The issue was now joined.

There was very possibly a strong personal element in Schmidt's sudden about-face on this issue, as well. He had aspired to be appointed to a new English-speaking professorship at Concordia Seminary. When this appointment was denied him, he became an ardent adversary of Walther and all that Walther stood for. This strong antagonism endured for the remainder of Schmidt's ministry in the Synod—and beyond, after he left the Synod.

Thus both of the original professors at the Synod's Luther Seminary took issue with the position both the Missouri Synod and the Norwegian Synod had taken on election.

*Alert One:* When a church body's theological faculty unanimously raises an issue, it is already (or becomes) an unavoidable issue. Both professors came directly out of the context (the Missouri Synod) with which they were taking issue; they both knew it well. The election issue was first raised almost immediately following the founding of the Synod's seminary, Luther Seminary, in 1876. This double professorial action should have put the Synod on high alert.

In good Lutheran tradition, theological professors at the church body's seminary are regarded as teachers of the whole church, or, in this case, of the church body they serve. They are much more than simple instructors of the future clergy. When a theological professor calls attention to a doctrinal or theological challenge, it needs to be considered carefully, seriously, and purposefully—not abruptly dismissed (as it was in this case). The professor's concern may be overturned, but only after due process.

## The Controversy Develops in the Synod's Districts

Professor Schmidt was a strong scholar, but less of a church leader. It did not take long, however, for the issue to come out into the open. The person who actually broke the issue of election publicly to the entire Synod was the district president of the Synod's Minnesota District, Pastor B. J. Muus. He did so at his Minnesota District's 1880 convention.

Muus was a dissenter and opponent by temperament; these characteristics were seen in several other instances where he seemed by instinct to take the contrary position. In this instance he took advantage of his elected position as district president. At the 1880 convention of his Minnesota District this subject was not on the agenda. Nevertheless, without warning Muus directed the major part of his presidential address at the convention to the doctrine of election. In doing so he broke with the Synod position and now openly and vigorously sided with the position of Professor Schmidt. His action took the convention completely by surprise. Muus had previously been a staunch Missourian and Synod mainliner. This was obviously an unannounced, public, agitating break with his previous position—and with the Synod.

Many delegates at the convention reacted negatively and challenged the propriety of what he had done. They acted by majority vote to eliminate this major part of his address from the minutes of the convention. They also acted to eliminate the discussion which followed from the convention record. Muus refused to honor either of these actions. His address was printed in its entirety as was the convention resolution, passed by majority vote, that his views not be included in the record, were private, and were not an official expression of the doctrine of election—nor an official part of the convention.

The fat was in the fire.

Muus had been both a prominent church leader and strong supporter of the Synod. He had also been a strong dissenter within the Synod on several key issues. And now he had perpetrated a more drastic break with his Synod colleagues by emerging as the principal leader of the opposition regarding the doctrine of election (or predestination).

This action of Muus would lead to his defeat for re-election as district president at a subsequent district convention, in 1883.

*Alert Two:* Muus, the district president, (as well as the professors) pointed out the already "built-in" nature of the conflict regarding the election issue within the Synod. All Synod members—both laity and clergy alike—had been raised and instructed in second form understanding of election ("election in view of foreseen faith"). Such instruction had come through Pontoppidan's explanation of Luther's Small Catechism, titled *Truth Unto Godliness*. The "built-in" nature of the conflict was that the Synod leadership was now teaching and promoting first form understanding of election—via their theological education and close association with the Missouri Synod—whereas the entire membership of the Synod had been reared in second form understanding of the doctrine.

Complicating the picture in the Synod was the fact that the Synod did not officially subscribe to the Formula of Concord, which actually defines election in terms of first form. The Synod subscribed (in good Dano-Norwegian tradition) only to the Augsburg Confession and Luther's Small Catechism among the seven specifically Lutheran Confessions, in addition to the three Ecumenical Creeds. The Norwegians sometimes referred to the other five Lutheran Confessions (of which the Formula of Concord was one) as the "lesser known" confessional documents. The members of the Synod, therefore, knew the explanation of the Catechism, *Truth Unto Godliness*, far better than the Formula of Concord.

## The Controversy in the Synod at Large

The leadership of the Synod, especially President H. A. Preus, wisely attempted to restrict discussion of election and related issues to the level of theological leadership and pastoral conferences. President Preus felt that public debate would be injurious to the church. (He was right.) To forestall public discussion and debate, Preus called for a colloquium of Synodical Conference leaders.

This meeting, held at Milwaukee, January 5-10, 1881, did not produce any definitive results. Thus, regretfully, this issue was now out in the open.

*Alert Three:* The Synod personnel who raised the issue were accountable for their negative behavior for the abrupt and crude way they raised the issue. The antagonists were all basically out of order. They made the issue personal immediately. Though it may be difficult in the church, challenges and issues should never be made personal. The antagonists should have been held accountable by the Synod leadership, which is a leadership role in any situation. By the same token, the Synod also should have held its own elected officials accountable.

Counter-arguments in a personal and hostile manner were equally out of order.

## The Controversy Develops within the Media

With the discussion of this subject out in the open, both the religious and secular press were filled with articles reporting and defending the two points of view. It became a ready topic of conversation and debate among church members and community people alike. Everything was fair game.

The religious press featured basically four periodicals. The Synod mainline cause was covered by (in translation) *Evangelical Lutheran Church News*, which was the Synod's official organ; and by *Necessitated Defense*, edited by Pastor H. Halvorson, who mainly refuted Schmidt's accusations against prominent Synod mainliners. The Anti-Missourians had two papers, both published by Schmidt: *The Old and the New*, begun in 1880, and *The Lutheran Witness*, appearing in 1882.

In the course of the conflict, by 1882, Pastor H. G. Stub, a staunch Synod mainliner and defender of first form, who was now a theological professor at the Synod's Luther Seminary in Madison, observed that the second form of the doctrine of election was "orthodox." In other words, it was acceptable. But, he added, second form was inferior to first form in that it attempted a rational explanation of what is a great mystery. Again we see the irenic impulses in the Synod. Professor Stub's observation should have been followed up by Synod leadership.

*Alert Four:* The basic Synod documents of the 1880s positively (if reluctantly) recognized the position and case of the Anti-Missourian Opposition, as well as the position of the Synod. What these papers make clear is that both forms were part of Lutheran theological and doctrinal history. Theological Professor H. G. Stub's statement of 1882 admitted that second form was not false or heretical, but incomplete. Pastor and District President U. V. Koren's statement (1884), "An Accounting," which became the official document of the synod pastoral conference, admitted the same; namely, that second form is not false or heretical, but inadequate and therefore dangerous.

Belatedly in 1910 (after the Election Controversy itself has passed) at least one of the Synod districts, the Eastern District, officially by convention action expressed the same position; namely, that second form was neither false nor heretical, nor a cause for division.

What all these Synod papers and documents admit is that both forms were part of Lutheran theological and doctrinal history. First form was confessional, which gave it special standing. Yet second form had been promoted by several Lutheran dogmatists in the seventeenth century, sometimes called the Lutheran Age of Orthodoxy; one of them, Johann Gerhardt, was actually termed "the foremost champion of Lutheran orthodoxy." Both forms were orthodox Lutheran.

In spite of the two forms, there remained only one Lutheran doctrine of election; namely, that God predestines individuals only to salvation, not to condemnation.

## The Controversy Expands within Broader Lutheran Circles

As early as 1882 Synod Pastor P. A. Rasmussen (an Anti-Missourian) spearheaded a movement to separate the Synod from the Synodical Conference. He attempted to work through the Synod districts; the general Synod convention did not take place that year. The move proved to be unsuccessful. But during that same year (1882) an incident took place which dramatically re-introduced the issue.

The regular convention of the Synodical Conference was held in Chicago on October 4 through 10, 1882. Among the delegates representing the Synod was Professor F. A. Schmidt. The convention denied him a seat, declaring that it could not recognize him as a brother in Christ.

Following this refusal, four colleagues who were Synod delegates (Koren, Stub, T. A. Torgerson, and J. A. Thorsen—all of whom had voted against him) issued a declaration stating that their action against Schmidt must not be taken to mean that they had broken fellowship with him in their own church body. (They were trying to be fraternal.)

Schmidt was not slow in pointing out the inconsistency of their position: How could their consciences permit fellowship with him on the synodical or congregational level, while according to Romans 16:17 they denied fellowship in the assembly of the Synodical Conference?

Schmidt and others (including P. A. Rasmussen) felt he had been unfairly treated. Rasmussen again appealed to the Synod—this time by letter to the congregations—to break with the Synodical Conference. The letter, though severely criticized by Synod leaders, was nevertheless timely and successful in crystallizing public support for withdrawal from the Synodical Conference.

In fact, so thoroughly was the climate of opinion changed that such staunch Synod leaders as H. A. Preus and U. V. Koren now began to advocate such a step, saying it would be good for the church body. The action to withdraw from the Synodical Conference was taken without serious opposition at the Synod district conventions of 1883.

During that same year (1883) the Synod's church council promoted a peace plan. The church council created a new chair at Luther Seminary in Madison. And the council called Pastor M. O. Bockman, an Anti-Missourian, to fill the new chair. The ratifying pastors' vote (which apparently was necessary in the Synod) was fifty-two in favor, thirty-eight against, with eighteen abstentions. The vote did not provide the required majority. Despite this, the council took the extraordinary step of extending a temporary call to the seminary professorship. Pastor Bockman declined the call.

It was unfortunate that this move did not work out. The filled professorship would have acknowledged and reflected the variety of positions within the Synod. It would have been a very timely move to promote peace. And Professor Schmidt would have had a like-minded colleague on the seminary faculty. In any event, the Synod council made a noble effort.

*Alert Five:* The "peace moves" by President H. A. Preus and the Synod leadership were absolutely commendable.

There were four specific "peace moves." President Preus' recommendation that discussion be limited to pastoral and theological conferences, his referral of the problem to the Synodical Conference, the Synod council's attempt to place a second Anti-Missourian theological professor on the seminary faculty, and finally (and conversely) the leadership's role in actually leading the Synod out of the Synodical Conference (in order to restore peace) were all timely and responsible actions.

The fact that none of these "peace moves" proved to be effective in solving (or stemming) the crisis was no reflection on the leadership. The failure, however, indicated that more urgent and extensive actions needed to be taken.

## The Controversy Develops Within Congregations

There were other unfortunate results of the Election Controversy within the Synod. In 1883 on Good Friday both President H. A. Preus and his son, Pastor C. K. Preus, were deposed as senior pastor and assistant pastor respectively by the Norway Grove Congregation in southern Wisconsin. Apparently Professor Schmidt (fifteen miles away at the seminary in Madison) was behind this move and undoubtedly the real instigator. This was a high-profile humiliation of the Synod president and his pastor son. The Synod responded by placing the congregation under church discipline for the next several years. The congregation eventually withdrew from the Synod in the latter 1880s and joined the Anti-Missourian Brotherhood.

In the long run there was a happy sequel to this event; the breach was healed thirty-five years later when the Norway Grove Congregation apologetically and readily and willingly called Pastor O. J. H. Preus, the grandson of H. A. Preus and the son of C. K. Preus as its pastor; he served there for ten years.

In 1885 veteran Synod Pastor J. A. Ottesen was deposed as pastor at Koshkonong, Wisconsin. Again it was a major humiliation for a true and faithful servant. Several families left the two Koshkonong congregations (East and West) as a result. Both congregations divided. East Koshkonong would be re-united in the 1960s—seventy-five-plus years later—and West Koshkonong remains divided to this day. Both Koshkonong congregations were involved in litigation in the 1880s to determine which groups owned the two church properties.

Sadly, many other congregations in the Synod also divided. Late in the Election Controversy another primary Synod congregation experienced schism. In 1889 the Lutheran Congregation in Decorah, Iowa, divided. Over 50 percent of its membership left to form an alternative congregation, which organized outside the Synod's jurisdiction.

The tragic irony was that this congregation was the "college church" of Luther College and informally the "mother church" of the entire Synod. The Synod had substantially subsidized the construction of this congregation's new "cathedral" church building in 1876, and the Synod would retain partial ownership of this building for the remainder of the Synod's history.

Once again there is a silver lining: In 2013 the two congregations, plus two more Decorah congregations founded during the twentieth century, jointly celebrated the sesquicentennial of the Decorah congregation's original founding in 1863. The celebration came 124 years after the 1889 division.

*Alert Six:* The unseating of pastors and the division of congregations revealed the extent of alienation caused by (or exposed by) the conflict.

Some congregational actions were flagrant and totally irresponsible. Congregational accountability was required; in fact, it happened in a few instances. It is possible the Synod did not yet have the district machinery in place to effect widespread problem-solving or accountability. These untoward congregational actions revealed the need to heal and re-unite. Reprimand and censure and discipline proved ineffective; they only drove the splinter groups further away. Often the congregational splinter groups were larger than the "loyal" groups, which then resulted in the splinter groups leaving the jurisdiction of the Synod.

Positive healing and re-uniting efforts, rather than negative actions, were required.

## The Controversy Expands to Other Doctrines

A further result of this controversy was that Pastor Muus energetically expanded the debate to include the doctrine of conversion. And Muus used this extension to further charge his opponents with Calvinism.

The controversy moved closer to a critical point at the All-Synod Pastoral Conference of 1884, held at Decorah, Iowa, in November. Here the mainline Synod pastors issued a document entitled "An Accounting," stating their position on grace, conversion, election, and assurance. The document was undoubtedly drawn up by Pastor U. V. Koren, the Synod's leading theologian. The document was signed by eighty-seven pastors (or 56 percent of those present).

The Anti-Missourian pastors refused to sign, met separately, and produced their own document entitled "Confession." This statement was signed by sixty-nine pastors (or 44 percent of those present).

*Alert Seven:* The crucial Synod Pastoral Conference (1884) revealed how evenly-divided the entire Synod was on this election issue.

The Synod-wide Pastoral Conference of 1884 was historically the "breaking-point" of this major controversy. No single party was able to carry the day. A slim majority (56 percent) of the clergy approved the stated Synod position. A strong minority (44 percent) took exception by not signing the Synod document. The minority also planned a schismatic conference for the following year (1885). The 56 to 44 percent split in the ranks of the clergy was a realistic "alarm bell" that emergency measures were needed to maintain the wholeness and unity of the Synod. Immediate action was required.

## The Controversy Leads to Serious Synod Conflict

The sixty-nine pastors who refused to sign the Synod document, "An Accounting," and instead drew up and signed "Confession," took a further step at the pastoral conference: They established an independent fund outside Synod control to help support Anti-Missourian church school and theological professors whose incomes might be in jeopardy because of their theological views. This "rump session" at the 1884 Synod pastoral conference was undoubtedly the breaking-point, plunging this group into outright schism.

Events now moved rapidly toward an open schism in the Synod. In 1885 forty of these Anti-Missourian pastors met at Red Wing, Minnesota, to take further action.

*Alert 8:* The Synod's strong emphasis on "rightness" and "correctness" and (conversely) "wrongness" also applied to the Anti-Missourian Opposition within its ranks; this emphasis backfired under the weight of a difficult challenge. "Rightness" was a worthy goal, which by-and-large the Synod achieved. Yet, in an internal controversy, "rightness" on the part of clergy and laity alike—the laity had also (carefully) been taught—produced enormous gridlock (to use a modern term). Both sides emphatically claimed they were "right." "Correctness," rather than pastoral concern and Christian respect for opponents, seemed to prevail on all fronts. Gridlock needed to be dealt with—biblically, pastorally, humanely—by all parties involved.

The Synod mentality may have been that the principle of the issue was more important than the people of the issue. In this case, principle trumped people.

## The Controversy Leads to Schismatic Action

When forty of the sixty-nine signers of the Decorah "Confession" met the following October at Red Wing, Minnesota, they took the following strong actions:

1) In an extreme statement, they demanded that heretical pastors and professors (those who had signed "An Accounting" at Decorah) be removed from office.

2) They recommended that "orthodox" (namely, Anti-Missourian) candidates of theology, denied ordination by the church council, seek it from the district vice-president or some other pastor.

3) They expressed the opinion that the presidents of the Minnesota and Iowa Districts (Koren and Harstad) be removed from office.

4) They condemned the official periodical of the Synod (*Evangelical Lutheran Church News*) as improperly representing the views of the church.

5) They granted a graduate stipend to a theological student with the hope he would enroll with the Hauge's Synod faculty at Red Wing, where Anti-Missourian "practical" students would be encouraged to study theology.

6) They voted $1,000.00 to be used as a salary for Professor F. A. Schmidt in the event he would be deprived of his regular salary.

A major result of the "rump session" (1884) and the follow-up meeting at Red Wing (1885) was that a schismatic auxiliary treasury was set up, which was beyond Synod control. Pastor B. J. Muus and a committee representing the three Synod districts were to supervise this fund, of which a layman from Decorah would be the treasurer.

*Alert Nine:* The renegade (Anti-Missourian) clergy's unreasonable demands (1885) and plans for an alternative seminary (1886) highlights a total synodical emergency. Shoring-up and unifying measures became an immediate necessity. As the Synod prepared for its forthcoming general convention (1887), unifying measures and actions needed to be the order of the day. Instead of planning stringent and censuring resolutions against the rebels, the right hand of fellowship needed to be extended. The Synod renegades needed to be recognized and re-claimed as brothers in Christ. The Synod's general convention at this critical stage (1887) should have been the ultimate in restoration and reconciliation—instead of reprimand and censure and separation. The convention should have been and done the opposite of what it actually was and did.

Moreover, the leadership of the Synod needed to remind themselves that they were the leaders and pastors of the whole Synod, not simply of those who were agreeing with and supporting them.

## The Controversy Leads to Synod Action

Reaction within the rest of the Synod was expressed by a pastoral letter from President H. A. Preus. He characterized the Red Wing action as schismatic. He was alarmed that it would subvert church order, undermine the constitution and institutions of the Synod, and encourage unionism.

When President Preus wrote to Pastor Muus requesting a list of the pastors and professors who were present and voting for the Red Wing resolutions, Muus refused to supply it. The Anti-Missourians reportedly felt that they were in a difficult logistical position. The mainline Synod leaders held all the major offices in the Synod:

1) The synodical president and all three district presidents were mainliners. (In mid-Controversy district elections, the three districts had all elected or re-elected mainline district presidents.)
2) The church council was controlled by mainliners.
3) Two of the three theological professors at Luther Seminary in Madison were mainliners.
4) The president of Luther College was a mainliner.
5) The editor-in-chief of the synodical periodical (*Evangelical Lutheran Church News*) was, too.

Apparently the Anti-Missourians felt their position was untenable. This was the mentality behind their strong actions at Decorah (1884) and Red Wing (1885). This would lead to further strong action in 1886.

It was clear that one of the places where the Election Controversy was most keenly felt was at Luther Seminary in Madison. Relationships in the faculty were not good. During the school year of 1885-86, Professor Schmidt did not teach. The enrollment declined from about twenty-five to only seven students. Of those who had transferred, eight had gone to Concordia, two to the Wisconsin Synod seminary at Milwaukee, and six (supposedly Anti-Missourian) to Capital at Columbus.

*Alert 10:* When a synod's institutions (college and seminary) are under siege, the depths of the synod's emergency is on display. Both institutions suffered significantly as a result of the Election Controversy. Both institutions did recover once the controversy was over. College enrollment, for example, soon returned to normal.

## The Controversy Leads to Opposition Response

Faced with this seminary situation, the Anti-Missourians decided to establish their own seminary. The action was reached at a private meeting in connection with the Synod's Iowa District Convention at Austin, Minnesota, in the early summer of 1886.

Pastor Muus was entrusted with the project. He reported back in August that arrangements had been made with the Board of Trustees of St. Olaf's School, of which board he was the chairman, to house the seminary. Professor Schmidt and Pastor M. O. Bockman were to be the two theological professors. The seminary would open that fall of 1886. (This seminary move upgraded St. Olaf's School to college status; it would change its name to St. Olaf College in 1889.)

The seminary at St. Olaf was called "the Lutheran Seminary" or more often "Lutheran Pastors' School." It operated as a private institution until 1890, when it was assimilated into the United Church Seminary.

*Alert Eleven:* The formation of an alternative theological seminary was definitely a schismatic act. Procedurally it was out-of-order. Respectful communications seem to have been entirely lacking in the lead-up to its institution. There is no evidence that civil negotiations within the Synod—and a resulting impasse—led up to it. Instead, it was abrupt and insulting. The action does not appear to have been a "last resort." Rather, it appears to have been a "first resort." The opposition seemed prepared to act summarily.

The schismatic action which founded the alternative seminary is contrary and foreign to the nature of the church, which by definition abhors schism.

## The Controversy Finally Leads to Schism

Obviously, establishing an alternative theological seminary was regarded by the Synod as an ultimate act of defiance. The Synod met in its general convention at Stoughton, Wisconsin, in the summer of 1887. Resolutions were drawn and adopted denouncing the founding of the seminary at St. Olaf:

> The Synod cannot but consider the erection of a new theological school at Northfield (a) as an act of opposition to break down the Synod's schools which have been established in accordance with its constitution . . . (b) as a breach of the Synod's constitution; (c) as an act which is in itself divisive. . . .
>
> Therefore the Synod cannot tolerate in its members that such activities be continued and must earnestly admonish those who have taken part in them to admit their error and withdraw from them.

Apparently there was no move toward reconciliation by the Synod leadership inside or outside of the convention.

Speaking for the opposition at the convention [the Anti-Missourians] was not Pastor Muus, but Professor Mohn, the principal of St. Olaf's

School. On the floor of the Synod convention Professor Mohn delivered a strong statement rejecting the actions of the convention and "the Missouri teaching in regard to predestination and conversion" in the schools of the Synod.

This was the actual breaking point—at the Synod's general convention in 1887. Professor Mohn's protest was signed by thirty pastors and twenty-seven lay representatives, totaling fifty-seven delegates at the Synod's general convention. The split with the Synod became a reality at a meeting later that year when the Anti-Missourians, with Professor Mohn presiding, decided formally to withdraw from the Synod.

Instead of organizing a new church body, the group formed itself into the "Anti-Missourian Brotherhood," with Pastor L. M. Biorn as president. By the next year, 1888, approximately one-third of the Synod's pastors and one-third of its congregations (with a total membership of 50,000) had left the Norwegian Synod. The Brotherhood's program was to support the seminary at St. Olaf and promote the college program.

*The Epilogue: Pastor B. J. Muus*

When the fateful schism in the Synod took place in 1887, Pastor Muus was not among those who withdrew. He, instead, displayed real churchmanship. In this respect, too, he was a dissenter.

Muus had led the fight against the Synod's position on election and conversion. He had been regarded as the *enfant terrible* by his opponents in the Election Controversy. And he had used his position as chairman of the St. Olaf Board of Trustees to found an alternative theological seminary on campus. Yet he himself chose not to withdraw from the Synod. At a meeting of the Anti-Missourians held at St. Olaf in June 1887, he urged those who had broken with the Synod to return to its fold.

Characteristically, Muus remained in the Synod out of principle even when his congregation left in 1887. He considered it his duty to stay, to fight for the truth (as he saw it), and to oppose false doctrine (as he understood it). His colleagues objected, saying that it was no use to remain when one was cut off from the opportunity to help. But Muus replied that love of God and neighbor compelled him to stay in the Synod. "What is required of us is that each one is found faithful at the post where God has placed him," he said. He was a stubbornly loyal churchman.

A decade later, in 1896, he was officially requested to leave the Synod by his Minnesota District—with the approval of the Synod leadership.

When he still refused, the Minnesota District ousted him from the Synod in 1898. He stated it was the most humiliating day of his life.

*Alert Twelve:* The formation of the Anti-Missourian Brotherhood presented an unparalleled "opportunity" for the Synod. The Synod could have viewed the Brotherhood as an opportunity rather than as a scandal or disgrace. The opposition party had consciously refrained from immediately forming a new and competing church body. Official negotiations at the highest level could have been initiated by the Synod with the Brotherhood.

If official negotiations had been undertaken (and this opportunity had been capitalized on), the Synod would have had the unqualified support of the number one renegade of them all, the one who sparked the opposition movement in its entirety, Pastor B. J. Muus. Muus had purposely remained loyal to the Synod and strongly urged his colleagues to do the same. The results could have been worthwhile and interesting.

Both groups could have restored fellowship. This whole conflict cried out for perspective. The doctrine of election was not central or crucial to the integrity of orthodox Lutheranism. In this respect Lutheranism was vastly different from, for example, Reformed theology, where it is crucial. Agreeing to disagree on a lesser theological issue could have achieved reconciliation and unity within the ranks of Lutheranism.

## The Controversy Ultimately Led to Unity

Three years after its withdrawal from the Synod, in 1890, the Brotherhood would join the Conference for the Norwegian-Danish Evangelical Lutheran Church and the Norwegian Augustana Synod to form the United Norwegian Lutheran Church in America.

*Alert 13:* The formation of the alternate church body in 1890, the United Church, called for recognition, fellowship, brotherliness, and negotiations at the highest level. In a partial sense, this came about. Both the Synod general convention and the United Church constituting convention that year (1890) embraced actions for negotiations with each other.

Historically, there would be a silver lining to the whole conflict. The Election Controversy did have the ironic effect of jump-starting the 1917 merger process. This effort would take longer than a quarter-century, but it would eventually be fruitful. And the Synod's influence in the process would be monumental.

## In Summary

Some non-theological factors undoubtedly weighed heavily and contributed significantly to the Synod-wide Election Controversy:

1) A significant psychological factor was the fact that the Synod clergy leaders were almost entirely aristocrats. They had come from the upper classes of Norway. Norwegian immigrants were very conscious of social standing. Aristocracy added to the clergy's prominence among their parishioners and constituents in the Synod itself, and it further commended them for their willingness to accept calls to the frontier. Aristocracy also afforded the clergy the best old world education, which further equipped them to be capable leaders.

    Yet, undoubtedly these very assets also, humanly, produced reaction, even rebellion, in the frontier ranks of the laity. It also rankled their fellow clergy who were not so "entitled" by background. The human reaction to strong leadership in general, and authoritarianism is particular, was something to be expected eventually. The reaction was very possibly a phenomenon waiting to happen.

2) A second psychological factor was the common Norwegian propensity to independence. This was so pervasive that it was often difficult to gauge or anticipate. Norwegian independence was a trait which German immigrants found difficult to understand. Synod colleagues in the Missouri Synod never were able to read or fathom Norwegian independence correctly.

3) Sociologically, a few congregational observations suggest that first form understanding of election was often supported by the more sophisticated—either by education in general, parish education, or social standing. Second form (by definition) was easier to understand by the "ordinary" frontier church member. Second form gave a simpler explanation to election. First form was not only confessional, but also definitely more sophisticated.

Not only was the Election Controversy the most traumatic and tragic episode in Synod history, but it also was probably the most unnecessary and avoidable. The "alerts" indicated in this chapter illustrate how avoidable it actually was. The unfortunate result of this disagreement was that one-third of the pastors, congregations, and membership (totaling about 50,000) withdrew from the Synod in the wake of the Election Controversy. Remarkably, the Synod would re-coup almost all these numbers in the next sixteen years in time for its golden anniversary in 1903. Enrollment at Luther College and Luther Seminary (both of which had suffered) also recovered.

The election problem could have been solved peacefully. Twenty-twenty hindsight reveals it. The Madison Agreement, which would come in 1912, proves it. The Synod could have accomplished in the 1880s what the 1912 Madison Agreement, with very focused Synod leadership, achieved some thirty years later.

CHAPTER ELEVEN

# Home Missions Before the Election Controversy (1864-1887)

In 1864—eleven years into the Synod's existence—the Norwegian Synod inaugurated a synodically supervised home mission program. In that year a mission committee of three members, responsible for promoting both home and foreign missions, was created.

This, however, did not launch what we today call "home mission" or "American mission" activity. Prior to this time devout lay people, pastors, and congregations had been seeking out and ministering to Norwegian settlers before synodical organizations had come into being. Outreach had gone on before anything resembling organized home mission work had been authorized. A large part of the typical frontier pastor's work was much like that of a home missionary.

The Synod engaged in home mission endeavor in widely-scattered fields. Its activity in the period of the 1860s, 1870s, and 1880s encompassed a greater area than did that of the other Norwegian Lutheran church bodies. It supported home mission projects on the East Coast, on the West Coast, in Canada, and in Texas. Major attention during this period was given to Minnesota and the Dakota Territory. In other words, a dynamic pioneer home mission effort was under way.

Because the Synod was throughout its history a pioneer church body, it considered immigrating Norwegian-Americans as its chief mission field. Home mission efforts tended to parallel Norwegian immigration.

In the 1880s, despite the strenuous efforts of the Synod and other Norwegian Lutheran church bodies, the church could not keep pace with the flood of immigrants that came to this country. Between 1880 and 1890 the Norwegian population in America increased by 125 percent, but church membership increased by only 67 percent. Only half of the influx was recruited by the church. However, during the next decade

(1890-1900) church membership more nearly kept pace with the increase in population.

The shortage of pastors in America had been a severe handicap right from the beginning. It restricted the amount of work that could be done and necessitated heavy burdens for the pastors. The Synod was in the forefront of strenuous efforts to recruit pastors from Norway, but Norway never supplied enough pastors to meet the needs of America. The Synod came under greater urgency—along with the other church bodies—to solicit and educate an American-born and American-raised ministry to alleviate the crying need for more pastors.

The Synod established a mission committee in 1864, and in 1876 the Synod was divided into three districts—Eastern, Iowa, and Minnesota. In 1879 each district accepted responsibility for home mission work within its borders, with each district establishing its own home mission committee. The common procedure for promoting home mission work was to call and support traveling home missionaries. Sometimes these missionaries were full-time employees of the Synod; sometimes they were part-time employees who were serving congregations of their own. In other instances, pastors got leaves of absences from their own congregations to serve temporarily in this capacity. The Synod—unlike other church bodies—always used ordained pastors for this assignment. This type of arrangement began for the Synod in 1868, when the Synod authorized the calling of its first traveling home mission pastor. The next year (1869) Olaus Normann was ordained as pastor of the St. Paul, Minnesota, parish to be a traveling home mission pastor.

The names of these traveling home mission pastors and their co-workers are legion, for a great many men were occupied with this work over the years. These home missionaries were expected to keep their Synod informed of their activities, and many of them faithfully did so in the columns of the synodical periodical.

The work of home missions was something everyone was expected to be concerned about. All pastors were expected to do what they could for the unchurched Norwegian settlers in their communities. The 1873 convention of the Synod went on record stating that pastors, especially those living on the frontiers, must regard it as their sacred duty to minister to those who were without pastoral services—or to endeavor to have them visited.

Congregations were encouraged to permit their pastors to devote a portion of their time to making trips to unchurched communities. It was customary for professors at the synodical schools and for theological students to engage in home mission work during their vacation periods.

The leaders of the Synod seem to have been strongly concerned about doing something for the spiritual needs of the thousands of immigrants. President H. A. Preus is a good example of a vigorous promoter of home mission work. His annual messages to the synodical conventions and his articles in the synod periodical reveal his interest and leadership. Preus is also a good personal example of a well-traveled mission emissary and founder of many congregations. Other Synod leaders were, too.

Interest in home missions was fostered in several different ways:

The synodical periodical published news and reports about home missions and the work being done.

Congregations were encouraged to have special home mission services with offerings for home mission work.

At the synodical convention it was the practice to devote a session and/or a sermon to the home mission cause.

Women's activities in the congregations gave highly valued support to the work of both home and foreign missions, and the formation of such women's activities was strongly encouraged.

Many obstacles confronted those concerned about home mission work:

1) There were too few workers for the task.
2) There was always a shortage of funds.
3) In many cases distances to be traveled were great, and Norwegian settlers were widely scattered.
4) The middle 1870s were a period of hard times—namely, the Panic of 1873, drought, and grasshopper plagues. The Synod membership rallied in a most commendable way to the assistance of those stricken by grasshoppers and drought. A Synod committee created to assist those in afflicted areas distributed gifts in southern Minnesota, in Iowa, Dakota, and Kansas.
5) The Election Controversy of the 1880s put a damper temporarily on support of home mission efforts in the Synod. However, when the controversy was over, the call went out for a greatly intensified home mission program.

The Synod's interest in carrying out a churchly and spiritual ministry among Norwegians in New York City and the surrounding area resulted in its undertaking two special home mission projects in that location: an immigrant mission and a seamen's mission. The name of Synod Pastor Ole Juul is prominently associated with the origins of both missions. In 1866 Pastor Juul accepted a call to serve the Synod's New York congregation. From this position he endeavored to minister to Scandinavian seamen who frequented the port in great numbers. The work prospered under him and a succession of pastors, but there were frequent financial difficulties. The pastors visited seamen in ships, hospitals, and boarding houses; held services in the seamen's church; distributed literature; and maintained a reading room. Beginning in 1890, the Synod provided annual financial support for the seamen's mission as a home mission project. Similar work of a less organized nature was at times carried on in other eastern seaports, such as Baltimore and Boston.

Pastor Juul felt a concern for helping the many immigrants who entered the United States through the New York harbor. At his suggestion the Synod in 1873 authorized the calling of an "immigrants' missionary" for New York. Peder B. Larsen, Juul's assistant in his work with seamen, was called to this position. Pastor S. Keyl of the Missouri Synod, who was already engaged in this work for his synod, was of great assistance to a succession of Synod workers; he made available to them office facilities and their hospice, called the Lutheran Pilgrim House. The missionary, besides conducting devotional services in the Pilgrim House, engaged in personal conversation with individuals, distributed tracts and books, and provided immigrants with the names and addresses of Synod pastors in the areas to which they were going or moving.

Synod parish pastors in New York City felt it was their assignment and challenge to locate and call on all the Norwegians who had settled and were living in New York City. It was quite a task!

In 1890 the Synod authorized a home mission project among Scandinavians in Mormon Utah. Forty-five years earlier, in the mid-1840s, pioneer Pastor J. W. C. Dietrichson had written about his concern over the inroads of Mormonism among Midwestern Norwegians. Now immigrants direct from Scandinavia as well as westward-moving settlers were enamored of Mormonism in Utah. The mission in Utah was a great effort for twenty-two years, but it did not produce many tangible results. The Synod regretfully abandoned this mission in 1912.

All this reveals that the period from 1864 to the Election Controversy was a time of growing awareness in the Synod of home mission responsibilities and of home mission activity. Many new fields were developed.

Many congregations and preaching places were established. But much of the work was not solidly grounded. The frontiers were still expanding, and the years following would see many additional areas settled. The result was that the home mission task was one that continued to grow in magnitude.

Although the period before the Election Controversy saw groundbreaking and fruitful beginnings in home mission work, twenty-seven remaining years of the Synod (1890-1917) saw a greater flowering of home mission activity and a much more remarkable growth in church membership.

CHAPTER TWELVE

# Home Missions after the Election Controversy (1890-1917)

At the 1890 general convention of the Synod, this resolution was adopted:

> The Synod acknowledges that the home mission is the mission lying nearest at hand and ought to be vigorously supported."

Norwegian-American immigration continued to set the agenda for the Synod's home mission program after 1890, and for the remainder of the Synod's history. Logically, linguistically, culturally, and with common church background, Norwegian-Americans were the people the Synod was best equipped to serve. The Synod was not prepared to minister to people of a different background.

## The Extent of Home Mission Activity

The frontier of Norwegian expansion, to the west and north, led out of the Midwest. It included northern Minnesota, the Dakotas, Montana, Canada, and the Pacific Northwest. These areas would be the greatest home mission challenges between 1890 and 1917.

The pull of migration also diminished the earlier Norwegian settlements as immigrants moved north and west. President Stub described the problem facing older congregations of the Synod in Illinois, Wisconsin, Iowa, and to a lesser extent Minnesota: ". . . year after year caravans have gone to North and South Dakota, Montana, the West Coast, and Canada."

For this reason, it is not surprising that the Eastern District of the Synod gave significant attention to the home mission program of the Synod. In 1895 the Eastern District budgeted $5,000,00 for that purpose—a goodly sum for that time.

Following 1890, the home mission programs of the other Norwegian Lutheran church bodies paralleled and competed with the Synod's. Yet, during this period the Synod excelled in home mission work.

From 1890 to 1917, the most concentrated home mission action was northern Minnesota, the Dakotas, northeastern Montana, and the prairie provinces of Canada. Settlement of the fertile Red River Valley had begun about 1870. Over a period of many years Norwegian immigrants continued to come in large numbers, thickly populating much of the region. The result was that northwestern Minnesota and eastern North Dakota became one of the areas of heaviest concentration of Norwegian Lutherans in the entire nation. (After the 1917 Grand Union this area was able to garner a huge percentage—50 percent—of the new NLCA's home mission program, due to an enterprising district president, who was a former distinguished Synod pastor.)

The line of the frontier steadily moved across the Dakotas in the last two decades of the nineteenth century (1880-1900) and into the early years of the twentieth century. Norwegian settlements and congregations were spread across the entire northern one-third of the state of North Dakota in an unbroken chain—following the route of the Great Northern Railroad—and spilling over into northeastern Montana. The western counties of North and South Dakota were settled by Norwegians after the turn of the century. The western Dakotas, especially south and west of the Missouri River, were described as late as 1917 as "almost entirely a mission field."

The tremendous growth in the number of congregations in these frontier areas was reflected in organizational changes in the Synod. The Minnesota District had previously extended all the way to the West Coast. It would be reduced geographically by two new districts: In 1893 the Pacific District was organized. In 1908 the Northwestern District—composed of North Dakota, Montana, Manitoba, Saskatchewan, and Alberta—was organized. Consequently, the drastically reduced (in size) Minnesota District was now confined to the state itself. Still, in 1916 District President Bjorgo was able to report that although the Minnesota District had become the smallest of the Synod's districts in geographical size, it was the largest in membership.

Interestingly, shortly after 1900, Montana was regarded as a particularly promising mission field. In 1911, District President P. A. Hendrickson of the Synod's Northwestern District over-optimistically expressed the opinion that Montana would eventually become as Scandinavian as North Dakota. The congregations were chiefly concentrated in northeastern Montana, to the area where Norwegian immigrants were flocking early in the 1900s. The congregations then extended westward across the northern part of the state to the Rocky Mountains, continuing a pattern of settlement characteristic of North Dakota.

In Colorado several Synod congregations and preaching places were established in the early 1900s, with one Synod congregation dating back to 1881.

On the West Coast there had been developments from the 1870s. After 1890 the stepped-up influx of settlers into Washington and Oregon resulted in expanded and intensified efforts by the Synod. The Puget Sound area saw the greatest concentration of Norwegians, and it was there that church work was most intensive. By 1891 the Synod had six pastors serving in Washington. When the Pacific District of the Synod was created in 1893, it included fifteen pastors: eight in Washington, two in Oregon, and five in California. The Synod's Pacific District required financial subsidies from the other Synod districts over a period of many years. It remained primarily a home mission district with a small membership. Early high expectations for home mission progress in the Pacific Northwest did not fully materialize, but it continued to be a home mission field of primary importance. Several congregations were organized by the Synod in Oregon and California; later some of these congregations and preaching places had to be discontinued.

Canada was the destination of numerous Norwegian settlers for two decades prior to World War I. Manitoba, Alberta, and especially Saskatchewan became the most Norwegian of the provinces. A Synod congregation was established near Northgate, Saskatchewan, in 1903. Earlier the Synod had carried on home mission work in the eastern provinces of Quebec and Ontario, dating back to 1862 in Quebec and 1876 in Ontario. By 1900 that work was suspended. Six Synod congregations organized in Manitoba in 1876 were taken over by the Icelandic Synod in 1885.

In Canada there seems to have been close home mission cooperation between the sister Norwegian Lutheran church bodies. Between 1890 and 1917 approximately 430 Norwegian Lutheran congregations of all church bodies (the Synod, United Church, Hauge's Synod, Lutheran Free) were organized in Canada, plus about 120 preaching places. In fact, an informal church body known as the Norwegian Lutheran Church of Canada came into being. In 1917, at the time of the Grand Union, there were 340 congregations and preaching places still a part of the Norwegian Lutheran Church of Canada. There were forty-nine pastors, six of whom were Synod pastors. Each pastor was responsible for an average of six or seven locations.

## The Organization of Home Mission Work

The Synod organization for home missions during this final period (1890-1917), a quarter of a century, was different from other church bodies, including the United Church and Hauge's Synod. Each district maintained its own home mission treasury. Each district president, in addition to his other duties, was a home mission superintendent and was paid from home mission funds. There was no general synodical home mission committee or synodical superintendent. This system worked effectively. During this period (1890-1916) the Synod excelled in home mission work.

After the Election Controversy of the 1880s and the resulting heavy losses of membership, the Synod put forth a strenuous effort and replaced most of its losses. To increase interest and to encourage financial support for home missions, the Synod made use of several avenues:

1) The encouragement of women's activities.
2) Annual mission festivals in each congregation or parish.
3) Offerings on special occasions.
4) Special mission services at synodical or district meetings.
5) Use of the synodical periodical to inform and publicize home mission news.
6) Encouraging Synod and district officers to take responsibility for stimulating interest and providing the necessary leadership.

In earlier years, a large number of pastors were engaged in home mission activities in their communities. In addition, pastors of established congregations, synod school professors, theological professors, and theological students did home mission work on a short-term basis, particularly during the summer months. Now, in this last quarter-century (1890-1916), the Synod set up a Church Extension Fund. The function was to provide new congregations with financial assistance for the construction of church buildings. In this program, the Synod led the way, The Synod set the example in 1892, and the United Church followed in 1897 and Hauge's Synod in 1910. At the time of the Grand Union (1917), President Stub reported that over a period of twenty-five years, 246 congregations had been assisted in church building. At the Grand Union, the Synod had $115,000.00 in its Church Extension Fund—compared with $40,000.00 in the United Church fund and $8,000.00 in the Hauge's Synod fund.

## Special Missions

A number of special mission enterprises were carried on by the Synod. They were regarded at times as foreign missions, though now (in hindsight) we would categorize them as home, or American, missions. These special missions were established to minister to Alaskan Eskimos, Norwegian Mormons in Utah, African-Americans ("American Negroes"), and American Indians. President H. G. Stub specifically called these activities "foreign missions."

The Alaskan mission was begun in 1894 when Pastor T. L. Brevig was commissioned by the Synod to serve as a missionary at Teller, Alaska. He also served as a school teacher there for the U. S. government. Brevig devoted twenty-three years to this difficult field, serving there from 1894 to 1917.

The Mormon mission in Utah was authorized in 1890. The work was actually begun in 1892 with the organization of a small congregation. The purpose of the mission was to reclaim Norwegians who had been won over to Mormonism. This Mormon mission attracted considerable support, but the work was difficult and the fruits meager. In the course of time this "foreign" mission was taken over by the home mission committee of the Iowa District. Eventually the Utah mission was discontinued in 1912, after twenty years of earnest but frustrating work.

The Synod undertook no work of its own among the African-American (then termed "Negro") population. But contributions from congregations and individuals were frequently sent to the Synodical Conference for its Negro mission.

Wittenberg, Wisconsin, was the site in 1884 for the beginning of the Synod's American Indian mission. For some years this was regarded as the chief "foreign mission" of the Synod. Special emphasis was placed on educational work for American Indian children. In addition to the work founder Pastor Homme, the Synod was fortunate to have the long-term leadership of layman Axel Jacobson.

The Seamen's and Immigrants' Mission of the Synod was begun in New York City in the 1870s through the leadership of Pastor Ole Juul. By the 1917 Grand Union, seamen's missions were maintained in New York, Boston, San Francisco, and Galveston, Texas. In each of these localities a seamen's pastor was of assistance to the Norwegian sailors by visiting them in ships, hospitals, and boarding houses; distributing Christian literature; conducting services; and maintaining a reading room. The seamen's mission assisted thousands of immigrants with counsel, encouragement, spiritual help, and (often) lodging. The Synod was the only body to conduct seamen's missions, although the United Church established an Immigrant Mission in New York City in 1906.

## Missions in the Inner City

Later Norwegian immigrants settled in larger cities, especially in Brooklyn, Chicago, and the Twin Cities. Also, many second and third generation Norwegian-Americans left the countryside for urban centers. In 1917, Chicago had between 70,000 and 100,000 Norwegians; Minneapolis had 50,000. The Synod had a number of city congregations, especially after the turn of the century (1900). It also supported city missions and missionaries, who assumed responsibility for chaplaincy, institutional work, and relief work. Historians have commented that this somewhat followed the European concept of the "Inner Mission."

The earliest city mission was organized by the Synod in Chicago in 1905, preceding other efforts by two years. City missions developed ministries in a number of needed areas—youth work, a rescue mission, a day nursery, summer camps for children, maintenance of an industrial mission, the distribution of food and clothing to the needy, evangelistic work, assistance in finding employment, and the operation of a bookstore. By 1917 the Synod was supporting city missionaries in Brooklyn, Chicago, Minneapolis, St. Paul, and San Francisco.

Synod Pastor Otto Juul made this statement in his report when he was serving in Minneapolis as city missionary in 1916-1917, and historians say this was typical:

> Up to the first of May I had visited the hospitals 101 times, and had shared the Word of God with about 800 patients; in addition I had made eighty house calls in carrying out my duties. I have been present in children's court once or twice a week, have been at the rescue home thirty-four times, and have frequently visited the jails and various charitable and

disciplinary institutions in and around the Twin Cities and have been of some assistance in procuring work for several people.

## A Sequel: Evangelism

Evangelism was closely associated with home missions. However, unlike other church bodies, the Synod believed that the parish pastor was the only evangelist required. Thus, the Synod made no provision for any type of synodically-promoted evangelism (in the congregation or the community), either by pastors or laymen.

In 1963, forty-six years after the Grand Union, this writer encountered a former Synod pastor who was hesitant to engage in his conference's evangelistic "Preaching—Teaching--Reaching Mission." He reluctantly agreed to do so only with the use of former Synod pastors or their descendants in his four-congregation parish.

## The Continuing Challenge

Home missions was both a cooperative and competitive effort with sister-Norwegian-American Lutheran church bodies. Between all church bodies involved, by 1890, 2,629 congregations and preaching places had been started. By 1916 (the last record), 6,764 congregations and preaching places had been started—a goodly increase!

Despite the heroic efforts with which all Norwegian-American church bodies had confronted the home mission challenge, they could not keep up with the pace of immigration: In 1914 only 25 percent of Norwegian immigrants and their descendants held membership in Lutheran congregations. Lutheran membership was 500,000 out of a Norwegian population of 2,000,000. By 1917 over 1,000,000 Norwegians had no church affiliation.

A huge home mission challenge faced the merged church bodies following the 1917 Grand Union.

CHAPTER THIRTEEN

# The Synod's Education Enterprise

A strong compliment to the Norwegian-American Lutheran community was paid by an outside external observer: "The educational enterprise flourished among the Norwegian-American Lutherans. They did more in the field of education than any other church group during their heyday."

The Synod, among Norwegian-American Lutherans, was particularly interested in education. The education enterprise was especially effective in the Synod. It endeavored, and largely succeeded, in putting a definite education program into effect. Part-and-parcel of the Synod was a theological position which required a thorough instruction of its members in the Bible and in Christian doctrine. Synod educational programs and efforts covered the whole range from elementary to secondary to collegiate to normal teacher training to professional theological education.

Sometimes the charge was made that educational concerns and programs were promoted to the exclusion of evangelism. This turned out not to be true; educational programs and evangelism actually proceeded hand-in-hand.

The Synod's concern for education embraced the conviction that secular subjects should be taught in a churchly atmosphere.

## Elementary Education

Synod pastors engaged in the controversy over the American public school, often called the "common school." Synod leaders regularly criticized in strong terms the American "common school," primarily because they regarded it as secular, inefficient, and unsuited to the needs of Norwegian-American pioneer children.

Synodical leaders and pastors preferred to establish a system of parochial schools, in which both sacred and secular subjects could be taught by teachers in the employ of the parish. This would make it unnecessary for their children to attend American public schools. In this enterprise, the Synod pastors found themselves generally at odds with the laity.

Consequently, the Synod's championing of parochial schools was largely ineffective. President H. A. Preus acknowledged this when he reported in 1888 that he had been arguing for parochial schools for twenty years, but had been a "voice in the wilderness."

However, Synod congregations did respond to Synod leadership by more generally following the practice of holding "religious" schools for a few weeks when public schools were not in session (for instance, in the summer). Some basic secular subjects might also be taught in these schools. The laity did co-operate widely in holding and promoting these vacation "religious" schools, and these schools generally were effective and successful.

Nonetheless, a few attempts were made with parochial schools. Of these, half-a-dozen stand out: Our Savior's in Chicago, Illinois; Madison, Wisconsin; Decorah, Iowa; Perth Amboy, New Jersey; Perry, Wisconsin; Lemonweir, Wisconsin, with five districts and five separate schools.

Once again, we see the will of the laity prevailing over their leaders, the clergy. By and large Synod people did not move away from public education. As always, the clergy gave good leadership, and the laity responded accordingly. As usual, the clergy proposed, and the laity disposed.

## Secondary Education (Academies)

With much more success, the Synod advanced the cause of secondary education. Many academies were founded by the Synod or by Synod constituents. These academies, which were room and board high schools, were a real avenue of service. In most cases they preceded the establishment of local community high schools and thus they filled a real need. They aided the church's young people and their families in ways that public high schools could not at that time.

President H. A. Preus in 1869 strongly advocated the founding of academies. The results were extensive and effective. Many thousands of young people were educated in these academies. They were a fine Synod enterprise.

The Synod maintained many more academies than any of the other Norwegian Lutheran church bodies. A partial list of the most high-profile academies of the Synod is as follows:

1) Luther College Preparatory Department, Decorah, Iowa
2) St. Olaf's School, Northfield, Minnesota
3) Luther Academy. Albert Lea, Minnesota

4) Lutheran Ladies' Seminary, Red Wing, Minnesota
5) Monona Academy, Madison, Wisconsin
6) Willmar Seminary, Willmar, Minnesota
7) Bode Academy, Bode, Iowa
8) Stoughton Academy, Stoughton, Wisconsin
9) Aaberg Academy, Devils Lake, North Dakota
10) Bruflat Academy, Portland North Dakota
11) Park Region Luther College, Fergus Falls, Minnesota
12) Glenwood Academy, Glenwood, Minnesota
13) Pacific Lutheran University (only an academy), Parkland, Washington
14) Clifton Junior College, Clifton, Texas
15) Grand Forks College, Grand Forks, North Dakota
16) H. A. Preus Academy, Albion, Wisconsin
17) Gale College, Galesville, Wisconsin
18) Wittenberg Academy, Wittenberg, Wisconsin

In addition to these, a number of other academies were founded, but were much shorter-lived. Many of them served their areas for a time, but were forced to close after a few short years of service. In some cases public high schools emerged and took their place. In other instances, students and finances were not as forthcoming as expected from surrounding congregations.

In contrast to the Synod, there were approximately a half-dozen prominent academies in all the other Norwegian Lutheran church bodies.

The record shows that about 27,000 young people were educated in just five of the Synod academies alone—exclusive of the academy departments of both Luther and St. Olaf. The high point of the academies was the year 1907. From then on they waned until the Great Depression (1929-1942), which ended most that had not already closed.

## Normal Schools

The Synod operated two successive normal schools for the purpose of educating and training teachers. These students would be prepared for teaching not only in the church's parochial schools and academies, but also in public schools. Normal schools were one more aspect of the Synod's high-priority education program.

Luther College maintained a normal department from 1865 until 1886, for a total of twenty-one years. Luther had been founded to educate clergy. But its program was very quickly broadened. The education of educators was a major part of its expansion.

The Lutheran Normal School, at Sioux Falls, South Dakota, was dedicated three years later, in 1889. The Synod had acted in convention the year before, in 1888, to establish the school. The Lutheran Normal School continued for twenty-nine years, until it was merged with Augustana College in 1918; this merger followed the Grand Union of 1917, which merged many institutions of the Norwegian-American Lutheran church bodies involved.

In 1887 a private normal school was begun in Wittenberg, Wisconsin, by Synod Pastor E. J. Homme, in connection with his many, fine enterprises. Shortly later Pastor Homme joined the Anti-Missourian Brotherhood, and the school went with him. It remained in existence for only three years, until the formation of the United Church in 1890.

## College Education

The Synod's crowning achievement was higher education, which became a major success story.

*Luther College*

Luther College became the most prominent and permanent among the Synod's many fine educational institutions. The Synod from its very beginning had made plans to found its own college or university. Luther College was founded earlier than planned on a post-haste, emergency basis in connection with the Civil War. The stress and strain within the Synod over the slavery issue hastened its beginning. Luther very quickly became intimately entwined with the fortunes, traditions, and emphases of the Synod.

Begun in 1861, Luther was moved by pre-arrangement to Decorah, Iowa, the following year. The main building was dedicated in 1865, at a cost of $75,000.00. The dedication was a major Synod event; reportedly 6,000 people were present.

Luther was an outstanding example of how a higher educational institution could both reflect and influence life in the church. A great power in the Synod, Luther set a strong example for other institutions in other church bodies. It paved the way for other colleges, and showed them the effect they could have within their own sponsoring church bodies. A prominent historian has pointed out: "The pride in, and affection for, Luther College that existed in the church body [i.e. the Synod] was remarkable. The school was truly the apple of the Synod's eye, and was soon exerting a profound influence on the pastors and laity of the church."

Luther College reached the age of 56 years under the Synod and has flourished right up to the present time.

*St. Olaf College*

A second institution begun under the Synod, St. Olaf College was known at its beginning as St. Olaf's School, it was founded and incorporated in 1874, opened in January 1875. Originally an academy, St. Olaf was not officially sponsored by the Synod. But it was founded and directed by Synod members as a private Lutheran institution. It depended on Synod congregations for financial support and student enrollment.

In the course of the Synod's Election Controversy (during the 1880s) the Anti-Missourian element of the Synod identified with St. Olaf. The Anti-Missourian seminary was operated on the campus from 1886 to 1890. During this same period, the transition to college status was made. The first collegiate class began in 1886, and the first college commencement took place in 1890.

*Park Region Luther College*

Located at Fergus Falls, Minnesota, Park Region Luther College was organized by the Synod in 1892 as a junior college and academy. Some maintain its founding was an effort to bring co-education into Synod higher education institutions. (Luther was a college for men until 1936.) In 1917 the junior college at Park Region was merged with Concordia College at Moorhead, Minnesota. This action followed the Grand Union of 1917.

*Pacific Lutheran College*

In 1890 the Synod congregation at Parkland, Washington, organized the Pacific Lutheran University Association. Four years later, in 1894, the association established Pacific Lutheran University. The Synod in 1890 had encouraged this move by adopting a convention resolution, which encouraged the establishment of a Lutheran high school in the West. The school retained its pretentious "university" name until 1899, when its was accredited as Pacific Lutheran Academy. Actually, it had never been more than a secondary school.

Following the Grand Union in 1917, Pacific Lutheran merged with two United Church institutions: Spokane College in Spokane, founded in 1907, and Columbia College at Everett, Washington, founded in 1909. The merger of these three institutions took place in 1920 to form Pacific Lutheran College as a junior college at Parkland, Washington. From there it developed into a "college of education," a liberal arts college, and finally Pacific Lutheran University (interestingly, its original name).

In the Grand Union of 1917, the Synod contributed significantly to two already established colleges: Concordia College at Moorhead, Minnesota, was augmented by its merger with the Synod's Park Region Luther College of Fergus Falls, Minnesota. A Concordia campus building continues to carry the name "Park Region." Augustana College of Canton, South Dakota, was augmented by its merger with the Synod's Lutheran Normal School of Sioux Falls, South Dakota. The newly-merged college was moved to the campus of Lutheran Normal in Sioux Falls.

## Theological Education

From pre-Civil War days (1857 or so), the Synod had educated its theological students at the Missouri Synod seminary, Concordia Theological Seminary, in St. Louis, Missouri. This arrangement lasted about twenty-one years, until 1878. Even after that year, some Synod theological students went to Concordia.

During the Civil War era and following, this arrangement was at times awkward; Missouri had been a slave state, and public opinion there had generally favored the institution of slavery. Adding to the awkwardness, Synod students at Concordia rarely felt they "fit in" socially with the German Missouri Synod students.

In 1876 the Synod took the first steps toward establishing its own theological seminary. From 1876 to 1878 the Synodical Conference attempted to form a seminary. When this attempt failed, the Synod proceeded on its own. In 1876 a motion in the Synod's general convention to transfer the "theoretical" department from St. Louis to Madison was defeated. But the decision was made to establish a "practical" seminary in Madison, Wisconsin, as soon as possible. The seminary began that same year, 1876. The "practical course" was to be provided for students lacking a college education or the pre-requisite classical training. It was to provide for students of more advanced age or special circumstances who could not acquire the normal academic pre-requisites.

Through the years until very recently, the ELCA's Luther Seminary in St. Paul, Minnesota, has dated its founding from this event in 1876.

In more recent years, Luther Seminary has dated its beginning in 1869, the year that Augsburg Seminary was founded. Augsburg Seminary was merged with Luther Theological Seminary in 1963.

The "theoretical "course, including the ability to use Greek and Hebrew, was continued at Concordia Seminary in St. Louis until 1878, when it too was moved by the Synod to Madison.

Professor F. A. Schmidt (who had taught at Luther College from 1861 to 1972 and at Concordia Seminary from 1872 to 1876) and Professor Ole Asperheim (who had taught at the Missouri Synod's Concordia "practical" seminary at Springfield, Illinois) were the two faculty members at the Synod's new Luther Seminary from 1876 to 1878.

Professor Asperheim, who had become a severe critic of the Missouri Synod, resigned in 1878. He was succeeded by Pastor H. G. Stub (the son of Pastor H. A. Stub, the second pastor of the Muskego congregation). Professor F. W. Stelhorn of the Missouri Synod was called as a third professor. When he declined the call, Pastor Johannes Ylvisaker was named to a professorship, which he assumed in 1879.

Luther Seminary remained in Madison until 1888.

The turbulent years of the Election Controversy (late 1870s and much of the 1880s) were trying experiences for the students. The controversy divided the faculty, producing friction between Professor Schmidt (who had suddenly become an Anti-Missourian) and Professors Stub and Ylvisaker (who were steadfast mainline Synod men).

When Professor Schmidt left the faculty in 1885 (after serving nine years, 1876-1885), harmony was restored. Pastor J. B. Frich of LaCrosse, Wisconsin (who was a Synod mainliner), was called to fill the vacancy.

In 1888 Luther Seminary was temporarily transferred to Minneapolis, and in 1889 it was located in suburban Robbinsdale. Its building was destroyed by fire in 1895, and it was housed in temporary quarters for four years. In 1899 it permanently occupied a brand new building, built especially for the seminary, in the Hamline section of St. Paul. Luther Seminary remained in that location throughout the final eighteen years of the Synod's history.

In 1917, at the time of the Grand Union of most Norwegian Lutheran church bodies, Luther Seminary was merged with the seminaries of the United Church and Hauge's Synod to form Luther Theological Seminary, St. Paul, Minnesota.

The Synod strongly emphasized quality theological education for its pastors. Because of this emphasis, theological professors were granted high status within the Synod itself. For this reason, the theological faculty of Luther Seminary was influential through the years:

In the early years:
> F. A. Schmidt
> Ole Asperheim
> H. G. Stub, who also served as Synod president (1910-1917)
> Johannes Ylvisaker

In the later years:
> J. B. Frich
> W. M. H. Peterson
> O. E. Brandt
> Elling Hove

The temporary teachers over the years at Luther Seminary were:
> T. A. Torgerson
> K. Bjorgo
> J. A. Ottesen
> Adolph Bredeson
> Bjug Harstad
> John Halvorson
> Professor John Dahle (for many years choir director and teacher of hymnody)

There were those who declined the call to the seminary faculty. In 1876, at the seminary's founding, the Synod choose pioneer Synod Pastor J. A. Ottesen as seminary president. He declined because he felt inadequate. In 1878 Professor F. W. Stellhorn of the Missouri Synod was called, but he declined the call. In 1883, at the height of the Election Controversy, Anti-Missourian Synod Pastor M. O. Bockman was called, but he declined the call.

The four seminary faculty members at the time of the Grand Union in 1917 were Stub, Ylvisaker, Brandt, and Hove. Each of these was destined to become a full professor at the new NLCA's Luther Theological Seminary. All did so, except for Professor H. G. Stub, who was chosen instead as the general president of the new NLCA.

The Synod's educational program was truly phenomenal for a pioneer church.

CHAPTER FOURTEEN

# The Synod and Foreign Missions

The beginnings of the Synod were closely tied to the Foreign Mission enterprise. All of the first three founding pastors—Clausen (arriving in 1843), Dietrichson (1844), and H. A. Stub (1848)—were considering possible calls to the South African mission field when they were re-directed to the Norwegian immigrants in America.

The Norwegian Mission Society (NMS) was organized just one year (1842) before the first congregation was organized at Muskego in 1843. And it was that year the NMS acted to call and support missionary Pastor H. P. S. Schreuder, with whom the Synod would become very closely associated.

A strong supporter of the NMS Schreuder mission to South Africa was Professor Keyser of the University of Oslo (Christiania), who later became the father-in-law of Pastor H. A. Preus. Preus had been strongly influenced by the mission interest of Professors Keyser and Kaurian, and later Professors Caspari and Johnson—all of the Oslo theological faculty. When Preus arrived in America, he began promoting foreign mission interest immediately in his Spring Prairie Congregation.

The first open expression of foreign mission concern came at the first preliminary Synod convention in 1851, when two mission offerings were received. At the second preliminary convention (1852), foreign missions was included as one of the stated purposes of the new Synod.

In the preliminary periodical, *Monthly News* (published 1851-52), Pastor Clausen contributed a number of articles on foreign missions. In one of them he deplored the devastating effect which the Napoleonic Wars had on the progress of missions. In the 1852 July issue of the *Monthly News*, one of the editors outlines the purposes of the Synod. Among them is "the sending of missionaries."

After the 1853 constituting convention of the Synod, the missionary program received increased attention. Though overwhelmed by pioneer pastoral responsibilities for an ever-increasing Norwegian immigration, many pastors still educated their members to interest and concern for foreign missions. Chief among them was Pastor H. A. Preus. As editor of the reorganized *Churchly Monthly News* (1855), Preus published news items from many foreign fields, especially the African Zulu mission under Schreuder. He was able to exert a wide influence for missions by virtue of his editorial policy.

During the early years of the Synod, mission work among American Indians was regarded as the chief "foreign mission" activity. They were the "heathen who lived nearest us." Consequently, when the first appeal to support the Indian mission of the Missouri Synod was reported in the *Churchly Monthly News* in 1858, it received ready support.

At the Synod general convention of 1859, a resolution presented by Pastor H. A. Preus was adopted which summarily stated that "the Church calls upon all its pastors and congregations to work for missions among the unevangelized, especially the Missouri Synod's mission among the Indians." This action by the Synod was "the first recorded synodical resolution which specifically urged the support of mission to the heathen." Pastor J. A. Ottesen was appointed mission treasurer. Pastor H. A. Preus and Professor Laur. Larsen were designated to lead the raising of funds for the American Indian mission of the Missouri Synod. Mission festivals in the congregations, special offerings in the Sunday schools, and mission offerings on confirmation and Epiphany Sundays were promoted.

In 1862 Pastor P. A. Rasmussen joined the Norwegian Synod. (He came from the Eielsen Synod and a few years of non-synodical affiliation.) His coming signaled a marked upgrade in foreign mission emphasis in the Synod. For the next twenty-five years Rasmussen and now-President H. A. Preus worked closely together in promoting foreign mission interest and concern in the Synod.

The Synod general convention of 1864, with President Preus presiding, adopted the following resolution: "The Synod must acknowledge that work for Mission, both among the heathen and among our countrymen is a task which has been greatly neglected by us, wherefore we urge congregations and pastors to work also for this cause.. To its advance the Synod elects a committee of missions consisting of three members." The committee elected to implement this action were Pastors J. A. Ottesen, P. A. Rasmussen, and B. J. Muus.

President Preus's reports to the Synod general conventions continued to call attention to the need of extending the Gospel to the pagans.

Again, he felt that the mission field nearest at hand was that of the American Indian.

President Preus set an example for the Synod in holding a mission festival at his Spring Prairie Congregation on May 20, 1865. Pastors Ottesen and A. Mikkelson joined him for the day. The offering of $67.00 was sent to the Missouri Synod mission for the American Indians. Similar festivals followed Preus's example in many Synod congregations. (The Spring Prairie festival continued annually for well over a century.)

During the biennium 1865-1867 a total of $1,410.52 in the Synod was contributed to missions. The primary amount of $1,322.50 was given to the Indian mission of the Missouri Synod, and $87.90 was sent to the Norwegian Mission Society (NMS) for the South African Zulu mission.

Emphasis on foreign missions continued to appear in articles in the Synod's periodical. The Indian mission of the Missouri Synod continued to hold first place in the program of the Synod until this mission was discontinued in 1868. The situation under which the Indian mission labored had become untenable. When the Indian mission was closed, Synod giving to the NMS work in Africa and Madagascar increased. In 1868 the Synod's revised constitution under "purpose" added the phrase "home and foreign missions."

In 1969 the NMSociety requested Norwegian congregations in America to cooperate with its work. The negotiations carried on between the NMS and the Synod resulted in the Synod's affiliation with the NMS that year. The Synod was the first of the Norwegian-American church bodies to affiliate with the NMS.

This request and action was the result of the NMS's expansion of its work in Madagascar. In 1861 the bloody queen of Madagascar died, and the chapter of the Martyr Church in that island was ended. The new queen sent out an appeal for missionaries throughout the Christian world. The NMS responded in 1866. The Madagascar enterprise had forceful repercussions in the Lutheran church in America in general, and in the Synod in particular. Increased interest and support of the NMS was the result.

At the Synod's general convention in 1870—held at Lisbon, Illinois, P. A. Rasmussen's parish—an offering was received for foreign missions. This was the first time since 1852 that the Synod recorded a foreign mission offering at its regular general convention.

The official affiliation of the Synod with the NMS was cordial. Pastor U. V. Koren represented the Synod, attending the general assembly of the NMS at Tromso, Norway, in July 1870. He preached the sermon at Sunday vespers in the Tromso church and gave a greeting from the Synod at the general assembly's closing session.

Relationships between the NMS and the Synod remained cordial until 1873. In that year, the Norwegian-Danish Conference was admitted into the same relationship with the NMS as that enjoyed by the Synod. This troubled the Synod, because it brought the Synod into back-door fellowship with the Conference; and the two bodies were not in official or ecclesiastical fellowship. During the 1870s no solution to this problem was found.

In spite of the troubled atmosphere, the Synod and its congregations continued to support the NMS. Mission interest and activity still persisted.

The NMS would not identify with either party in the Synod-Conference controversy. The NMS strove to maintain the affiliation of both church bodies. Moreover, there was disagreement within the Synod as to what needed to be or could be done.

The action taken by the Synod at its 1881 general convention constituted no decision. In an adopted resolution submitted by Pastor U. V. Koren, the Synod simply left it up to each individual congregation to decide what its attitude toward the NMS would be: Each congregation could support, or not support, the NMS as it wished. Many congregations continued to send offerings to the NMS. And to strengthen this support, the resourceful Pastor P. A. Rasmussen published a devotional and missionary magazine (1877-1887).

After the changed relationship with the NMS (1873), the Synod decided to support the Negro mission of the Synodical Conference, a mission organized in 1877. The Synod also acted to affiliate in 1877, and continued its support until 1890. However, after the NMS issue was settled (1881), contributions to the Negro mission dwindled.

## South Africa

Also coinciding with the changed relationship with the NMS, the Synod began to focus intensely on a mission parallel with the NMS. The foreign mission which held the greatest love for the Synod after 1873, and especially after 1882, was the Schroeder Mission among the Zulus in South Africa.

In 1873 missionary Pastor H. P. S. Schreuder severed his connection with the NMS. His relationship with the NMS had always been strained;

he had wished to represent the state Church of Norway rather than the NMS. But because it was not the purpose of the state church to send out foreign missionaries, Schreuder had accepted the call of the NMS and served under its auspices for thirty years (1843-1873). Along with his high-churchly tendencies, Schreuder was also strong-willed. The NMS was, in the main, a people's mission. Following his decision to become independent of the NMS in 1873, this strong-willed missionary would be supported by a Committee for the Mission of Schreuder, with headquarters in Oslo (Christiania).

The Synod, with its high-churchly orientation, found Schreuder to be a very congenial colleague. After 1873 it became involved in supporting the new Committee for the Mission of Schreuder. This interest in South Africa became personal when Professor Laur. Larsen, the president of Luther College, married Ingeborg Astrup in Norway in 1872. (Larsen's first wife, Karen, had passed away the year before, in 1871.) Mrs. Ingeborg Astrup Larsen was the sister of Pastors Nils and Hans Astrup, who had gone to Zululand from Norway as missionaries (with their families) in 1883 and 1884 respectively. They came to replace Schreuder and to assume responsibility for the Schreuder Mission among the Zulus. (Schreuder had passed away in 1882.)

Another link in the direct Synod relationship with the Zulu mission was made in 1890, when three young men from missionary families in South Africa came to Luther College as students. They were Johannes Astrup, the son of Bishop Nils Astrup; Carl Doving, a protégé of Bishop Astrup; and Heinrich Otte, the son of Missionary Carl Otte.

In 1892 Missionary Hans Astrup and his wife, Thekla Breder, who was a niece of President H. A. Preus, visited a large number of Synod congregations. Congregational offerings during their visit were very generous. In February 1893, the Committee for the Mission of Schreuder gratefully acknowledged this support and offered the Synod a voice in the committee. The Synod did not find itself able to accept this offer immediately, but recommended that Synod congregations continue their strong support.

In 1896 Synod President U. V. Koren reported that a committee had been chosen "to take care of this matter"—presumably official Synod support of the committee. Professor Laur. Larsen was the leading member of the Synod committee. Although he was the Luther College president, "no activity of the Church received a stronger support from him than foreign missions," according to his daughter, Dr. Karen Larsen. Two other Larsen daughters, Marie in 1893 and Hannah in 1896, went to Africa as teachers. Larsen's son, Pastor N. Astrup Larsen, became a missionary to China in 1913.

College and seminary students Johannes Astrup and Heinrich Otte (who would return to South Africa as missionaries), plus Marie and Hannah Larsen (who became missionary teachers), would place the Synod in the forefront of sending Norwegian-American Lutheran missionaries to the foreign field.

## Australia

Another mission project undertaken by the Synod before the Election Controversy was outreach to the Norwegian settlers in Australia. The Synod officially called Pastor L. Carlsen to this work in 1879. Pastor Carlsen left for that field the same year. He established several congregations and preaching places in Australia. However, when he returned to the United States in 1887, no provision was made for a successor.

After again visiting Australia for about a year, Carlsen returned permanently to the United States in 1891. Efforts to replace him did not materialize.

## The Intersynodical Missionary Conferences (1883-1890)

As previously stated, the relationship between the Synod and the NMS improved after 1881. A number of congregations continued to send offerings to the NMS. But individuals within the Synod and other Norwegian Lutheran church bodies had for several years felt an increasing need for separation from the NMS and for the formation of a common American organization to focus foreign mission interest. There was a growing desire for an inter-synodical missionary society. A series of intersynodical missionary conferences were held in an attempt to solve this problem.

It must be pointed out, however, that the chief purpose of these conferences would be to give instruction about the mission fields and their needs, as well as to cultivate mission interest to an even greater degree. Distinguished Synod Pastor P. A. Rasmussen was the dynamic force in this movement and the acknowledged leader.

The first intersynodical missionary conference was held at Rasmussen's congregation in Illinois in 1883. Dr. Christian Borchgrevink from Norway, a Madagascar missionary of the NMS, was the guest speaker. Four Lutheran groups were represented: ten pastors from the Synod, fifteen from the Norwegian-Danish Conference, two from the Norwegian Augustana Synod, and one from Hauge's Synod. Though the agenda discussion was planned on the question of establishing an intersynodical missionary society, Dr. Borchgrevink discouraged such a move. He instead urged continued support for the NMS and its extensive fields in Africa and Madagascar. The discussion of a proposed intersynodical missionary society was placed on hold until the next year. (Actually, it never came about.)

The second Intersynodical missionary conference was held at the North Prairie Church in Fillmore County, Minnesota, in 1884. The Synod was the best represented with seven pastors and twelve laymen, a majority with nineteen present. The Conference had eight, Hauge's Synod had seven, and the Norwegian Augustana Synod had two in attendance.

The third Intersynodical missionary conference was held at Eau Claire, Wisconsin, in 1886, with Conference President Gjermund Hoyme and Pastor U. C. S. Hjermstad as hosts. Again stress was given to supporting the NMS, especially extending the Madagascar field southward. The discussion noted that the Norwegian-American Lutheran support of foreign missions had increased to the point of calling and sending American young men to the mission field. (The Conference had just called its first missionary.)

The fourth Intersynodical missionary conference was held in the new home of the Synod's Indian mission at Wittenberg, Wisconsin, in 1887. Pastor A. Valen, a Norwegian missionary to Madagascar, was the guest speaker. Once again, continued support of the NMS prevailed. The upsurge of foreign mission interest in all the church bodies was noted with appreciation.

The fifth intersynodical missionary conference took place in Greenfield, Minnesota, in 1888. Pastor Peder Dreyer's congregation was the host. Missionary S. E. Jorgenson of Madagascar was the guest speaker. The recent schism in the Synod (1887) as a result of the Election Controversy was apparent; no Synod representative was present. This was the only mission conference in which the Synod was not represented.

The sixth Intersynodical missionary conference was held in Estherville, Iowa, in 1889. Particular interest focused on the China mission field at this conference. Daniel Nelson, an Iowa farmer and future great missionary to China, urged immediate action. The following year (1890) Nelson himself went to China, the first Norwegian-American Lutheran to do so.

The seventh and final intersynodical missionary conference was held in Story City, Iowa, in 1890. Officers elected at this meeting were leaders in the four church bodies. Professor H. G. Stub from the Synod was elected. Pastor P. A. Rasmussen, recently of the Synod, later of the Anti-Missourian Brotherhood and currently of the United Church, was also elected. Rasmussen had spearheaded these seven conferences.

These conferences had served a real purpose: They had united divergent synodical forces into one great mission purpose. They had stimulated missionary interest and zeal in all the cooperating church bodies. They had served as a means of expression for all who were impatient and dissatisfied with the hesitancy of the church bodies to become fully engaged in foreign missions.

They did perform a type of continuity until the church bodies themselves individually took responsibility for the foreign mission challenge.

## The Synod American Indian Mission

The interest in American Indian missions was revived in 1883, when the Synod began its own missionary program among the American Indians at Wittenberg, Wisconsin. Pastor Even J. Homme of Wittenberg had suggested that the Synod purchase land and call a missionary to this work. Erik O. Morstad was called to serve, and he responded by living in the log mission house near Wittenberg with five Indian children, and later six more, during 1884-1886. Pastor Homme then purchased the land where the mission became permanently located. Pastor Tobias Larsen was called as pastor of the local congregation and as Indian missionary. He was assisted by Professor Axel Anderson, who came in the spring of 1888. It became known as the Bethany Indian Mission. "There [Professor Anderson] remained for the rest of his life and made a great contribution to the Christian education of the Indians of Wisconsin," according to his successor. Many other pastors and lay people served faithfully in this effort.

Once this work among the Indians began, the congregations of the Synod rallied to its support.

The Indian mission for a time assumed the place of first importance in the Synod as far as "foreign mission" interest and support were concerned. The Election Controversy produced a dispute over the ownership of the Indian mission property, but the final agreement placed the property in the Synod's hands.

## The Anti-Missourians

The Anti-Missourian revolt and departure from the Synod (1887) was a hard blow against the program of foreign missions. Many of the dissenters had been the Synod's staunchest champions of world mission work. It took time for the Synod to rally from this setback. Thankfully, it proved to be a temporary setback. The Synod was challenged, in the wake of this tragedy, to move ahead significantly in both the areas of world and home missions.

## Alaska

In 1894 the Synod began its Alaska mission. Pastor and Mrs. T. L. Brevik were called to minister to the Lapps and Eskimos. It was heroic work. The mission continued for several decades. At its beginning the Synod considered its Alaska mission a "foreign mission." Eventually it was re-classified as a home mission program.

## Japan

In 1899 the Synod acted to begin mission work in Japan. In 1900 the Synod sent Dr. J. R. Birkelund, also an ordained pastor, to Japan as a medical missionary. Birkelund had previously served as an independent missionary to Japan (1892-1897). He pleaded Japan's cause at the Synod's district conventions in 1897. The Synod responded by sending him as its first missionary to Japan three years later, when he had completed his M.D. degree. Unfortunately, the effort proved to be abortive. Dr. Birkelund was forced to return home in 1902 because of the illness of his wife, and the Synod could find no one to replace him.

Almost a half-century later, in 1949, the Synod's successor church body (the Norwegian Lutheran Church in America/Evangelical Lutheran Church) would once again sponsor foreign mission work in Japan.

## China

In 1912 the Synod decided to begin a mission in China. Significant interest had developed among the students at Luther Seminary. The Student Missionary Society at the seminary offered to pay the salary of a missionary if the Synod would begin a new field. Synod President H. G. Stub warmly endorsed the plan and pleaded earnestly with the Synod to establish this work. The Synod decided to open a new field in China and called Pastor George O. Lillegard as the first Synod missionary to China. Pastor N. Astrup Larsen was called a year later, in 1913. Dr. J.

R. Birkelund was appointed Synod mission secretary; he also served as president of the Synod Board of Foreign Missions (1911-1917).

The Synod mission in China had a brief history (five years), as the Grand Union took place a short time later (1917). It then became a part of the unified mission field of the three merging church bodies, which was named the Lutheran United Mission.

## A Summary of Synod Support for Foreign Missions

*From the Beginning Through the Election Controversy*

Several of the earliest founders and leaders of the Synod had aspired to be foreign missionaries from Norway to Africa, before being re-directed to the needs of the American frontier. The early leaders fostered attention and concern for foreign missions in Synod congregations. The result was very early interest and support for missions, which developed over the course of this period. During the 1860s Synod attention and funds were directed to the work among the American Indians sponsored by the Missouri Synod.

The nineteenth century spiritual awakening in Norway precipitated interest in foreign missions and resulted in the formation of the Norwegian Mission Society (NMS). The Synod joined the NMS in 1869, and it was the first Norwegian-American Lutheran church body to affiliate with the NMS.

After 1873 the Synod supported the Schreuder Mission to South Africa in its mission to the Zulus.

During 1877-1890 many Synod congregations supported the Synodical Conference mission among African-Americans.

In 1879 the Synod authorized a mission to the Norwegian settlers in Australia—with some good results. After 1891 this mission had to be discontinued because replacement pastors were not available.

In 1884 the Synod launched a mission among the American Indians at Wittenberg, Wisconsin, which became permanent. For a while this was regarded as the chief "foreign mission" field of the Synod.

During this period, the Synod extended extensive mission education and information to its members. Although the Synod did not assume responsibility for a mission field of its own, neither did any other Norwegian-American Lutheran church bodies. (The exception may be Australian mission, which was officially a Synod project.)

*From the Election Controversy to 1917*

In this period there was a high degree of rapidly developing interest in foreign missions on the part of the Synod, as well as among the other Norwegian-American Lutheran church bodies. This interest was the result principally of the following:

1) The inter-synodical mission conferences of 1883-1890.
2) American visits of NMS missionaries.
3) The special work of Pastor P. A. Rasmussen.
4) The publicity of foreign missions in the Synod periodical.

In this period Synod congregations and members were principally supporting two foreign mission societies based in Norway: the Norwegian Mission Society (NMS), which sponsored mission fields in Africa and Madagascar, and the Committee for the Mission of Schreuder, with work among the Zulus of South Africa.

In 1900 the Synod began mission work in Japan. It had to be discontinued.

In 1912 the Synod began mission work in China.

The Synod's American Indian Mission at Wittenberg, Wisconsin, continued.

In 1894 heroic mission work was authorized by the Synod in Alaska, among the Lapps and Eskimos.

*After the Grand Union in 1917*

In August 1917, following the Grand Union, the three synodical mission fields in China (Synod, Hauge's Synod, United Church) merged to form the Lutheran United Mission of the Norwegian Lutheran Church in America (NLCA). The three fields were in the north-central section of China, in the provinces of Honan and Hupeh (with a total population of 7,000,000). The missionaries of the three church bodies (ninety-four of them) knew each other well; they had already engaged in a number of cooperative activities. By 1917 the pioneering period of the China mission was over. A substantial program of education, evangelism, and medical missions was now established.

In the Madagascar mission field, inherited from the United Church, there were thirty-four missionaries.

In the Grand Union, the newly merged church body (NLCA) accepted responsibility for the continued support of the Schreuder Mission to the Zulus in South Africa, which had been the Synod's main interest (and support). Ten years after the Grand Union, in 1927, the NLCA assumed full responsibility for the Zulu field.

The Synod mission among American Indians, which the Synod had once regarded as its chief "foreign mission" field, was transferred to the jurisdiction of the Department of Home Missions.

Likewise, the Synod's Alaskan mission among the Eskimos and Lapps, which originated as a "foreign mission," was transferred to the jurisdiction of the Department of Home Missions.

CHAPTER 15

# Social Ministry Institutions

The twenty-fifth anniversary of the Synod in 1878 marked the jumping-off point, after which formal, authorized, and organized charitable work began under the auspices of the Synod. Institutional and authorized charitable institutions did not immediately develop in the Synod. This lack of development exasperated Synod leaders. Yet, when it came, it flourished in quite remarkable ways. However, prior to authorized and organizational development of social service institutions, charitable work had been practiced on a large scale and widespread basis by Synod members in their local congregations and communities.

Some illustrations of effective, Christian, humane services rendered by Synod members consisted regularly of the following:

1) Kindness and compassion to the American Indians, which incidentally avoided many battles with the Indians later.

2) Help in clearing land for cultivation and inhabitation for newcomer immigrants from Norway or other locations.

3) Community and congregational help in the construction of new cabins for newly-arrived immigrants. Some observers noted how quickly the new homes were constructed by local congregational members.

4) Providing home hospitality for many kinds of need in the congregation and/or the community.

5) Widespread acceptance of newly-orphaned children into their homes (as *bona fide* family members) in the face of family tragedy.

6) Adopting orphaned children, who were moved in from other locations, and making them full family members.

7) Making room for the traveler or stranger, with the understanding that there was always room for one more.

8) Taking care of the sick and dying in their homes in the face of the multitude of frontier diseases—pneumonia, cholera, diphtheria, small pox, etc.
9) Generally making sure that all frontier, illness, and accident needs were met by those who were on location.

Christian hospitality and charity was the rule-of-thumb in early Synod congregations under the instruction of the scriptures and the church.

In 1878, at the celebration of the Synod's twenty-fifth anniversary. President H. A. Preus deplored the fact that nothing had been done thus far about establishing institutions to care for the needy and unfortunate. The need for such institutions had been felt for many situations and for some time. The Synod Missions Committee recommended that each district of the Synod select a committee of three members to determine what institutions were most needed and where they should be located. However, no action was taken on those recommendations at that time.

Two years later, Pastor Ole Juul, writing in 1880, stressed the need for an orphanage and a home for the aged. In that same year he recommended that the Eastern District establish a children's home in the vicinity of Wittenberg, Wisconsin. However, the district referred the matter to a committee. Pastor E, J. Homme, a Synod pastor in Wittenberg, had long favored establishing a children's home. When Synod action was not immediately forthcoming, and there was no response to the promptings of Pastor Juul and himself, he went ahead on his own initiative. Homme bought the necessary land in the little town of Wittenberg, where he was serving, and proceeded with plans for a building. President Preus strongly recommended support for this project. But the Synod was willing to go only as far as commending Homme's undertaking to its congregations, encouraging their support through prayers and gifts. The Synod wanted this Wittenberg project to continue as Homme's private undertaking, since it did not feel able to assume financial responsibility. In addition, there was some question about the advisability of locating a Synod institution on the "outskirts" of Synod territory.

A two-story frame building, located in the town of Wittenberg, was dedicated as an orphanage on Reformation Day, October 31, 1883. But over a year earlier, in August 1882, the work had begun, caring for four children and an elderly man. That year, 1882, is the date Lutheran Social Services of Wisconsin lists as the beginning of its operation and history.

Pastor Homme also established a printing press and published a paper entitled (in translation) *For Old and Young.* The surplus receipts were to be used for the home. He was a firm believer in the printed word, and he was responsible for other publications, including a Sunday school paper.

Homme expanded his program extensively and did considerably more building. He erected a building to assist in mission work among American Indians. An addition was made to the parsonage to serve as an academy. In 1887 he began to conduct a normal school for the training of teachers. The orphanage building in Wittenberg became too small, and in time Homme constructed a new children's home one and a half miles northeast of Wittenberg. The new building, although not fully completed, was put to use in 1898. And the original children's home in town became a home for the aged. Homme, however, had been caring for the aged prior to this time. In 1886, for example, he had in his care sixty-four children and eleven elderly people.

There were, therefore, four institutions at Wittenberg: a children's home, a home for the aged, a mission school for American Indian children, and a normal school. In 1887 an academy also was founded, but it was short-lived. Homme's institutions were supported by Norwegian-American Lutherans of all church bodies. The properties remained his personal possession during his lifetime. Upon his death, his institutions became the property of the United Church. Historians comment that Homme's philanthropy was outstanding. He was a real role-model.

However, Homme broke with the Synod during the Election Controversy, throwing his lot with the Anti-Missourians. After Homme identified himself with the Anti-Missourians, the Synod no longer felt it could commend his orphanage to its congregations.

The three Synod district conventions in 1888 considered the possibility of establishing a Synod children's home. And they laid the problem before the Synod church council. The church council decided upon the operation of a children's home in Madison, Wisconsin. In the fall of 1888 Luther Seminary had been moved from Madison to Minneapolis. This meant that the buildings in Madison, which had been used as an orphanage prior to the time when the Synod purchased them for seminary use, were again available for their original purpose. In the fall of 1889 a children's home was opened; and during the first year twenty-two children were helped. In 1894 the home was moved to a location just outside Stoughton, Wisconsin. The establishment of this home was a major Synod event. Reportedly, 3,000 people were present at the dedication service.

Unlike the home established by Homme at Wittenberg, the Martin Luther Children's Home was owned outright and operated by the Synod. Thus the Synod was connected with the first two Norwegian-American Lutheran children's homes.

Meanwhile, in 1890, the Synod Mission Committee called the attention of the Synod to the need for a home for the aged. The committee recommended that the church council ascertain what could be done about establishing one. However, there is no record of any action being taken at that time.

In the generation after 1890 there was a great deal of activity directed toward providing for badly needed institutions of mercy—long hoped for but only belatedly realized. By 1914 the Synod was affiliated with five of the twelve Norwegian-American Lutheran children's homes—more than any other church body. The Synod was affiliated with two of the seven Norwegian-American Lutheran homes for the aged—a number equaled by two other bodies. Many children's homes and homes for the aged of the Norwegian-American Lutheran church bodies were founded after 1890.

From Europe had come the concept of "Inner Mission" and the responsibility of the church and church people for homeless children, the aged, the sick, and the destitute. "Inner Mission" had been defined by one church leader as "the collective and not isolated labor of love which springs from faith in Christ, and which seeks to bring about the internal and external renewal of the masses within Christendom who have fallen under the dominion of those evils which result directly or indirectly from sin. . . ."

## Children's Homes

The Synod founded four children's homes—Homme Home (1882) at Wittenberg, Wisconsin; Martin Luther Home (1889) at Madison, later Stoughton, Wisconsin; Wild Rice (1898) at Twin Valley, Minnesota; Parkland (1900) at Everett, Washington. In addition, a Synod-related children's home was established in 1915 at Brooklyn, New York. Synod people and congregations supported many other children's homes.

## Homes for the Aged

The Synod founded three homes for the aged—Skaalen (1900) at Stoughton, Wisconsin; Josephine (1908) at Stanwood, Washington; and Glenwood (1914) at Glenwood, Minnesota. Six more were independent, but Synod related: Norwood Park (1896) at Chicago, Illinois; Norwegian Christian (1902) at Brooklyn, New York; Bethesda (1910) at Chicago, Illinois; Northwood ((1910) at Northwood, North Dakota; Lungblomsten (1912) at St. Paul, Minnesota; Ebenezer (1916) at Minneapolis, Minnesota.

## Hospitals

Three hospitals were founded by the Synod: Lutheran (1894) at Sioux Falls, South Dakota; Lutheran (1899) at LaCrosse, Wisconsin; and St. Paul (1901) at St. Paul, Minnesota. The following Lutheran hospitals were independent, but Synod-related: Norwegian-American (1896) at Chicago, Illinois; Deaconess (1899) at Grand Forks, North Dakota; St. Luke's (1903) at Fergus Falls, Minnesota; Good Samaritan (1910) at Rugby, North Dakota; Wittenberg (1911) at Williston, North Dakota; Central Iowa (1914) at Story City, Iowa; Dawson Surgical (1915) at Dawson, Minnesota; Luther (1915) at Watertown, South Dakota; Fairview (1916) at Minneapolis, Minnesota; and Moe (1917) at Sioux Falls, South Dakota.

## Deaconness Homes and Hospitals

During the 1880s and 1890s, three Lutheran Deaconess Homes and Hospitals were formed--- all with Synod affiliation, cooperation, or member support: Lutheran Deaconess Home And Hospital (1883) in Brooklyn, New York was the first. The leadership of Deaconess Elizabeth Fedde is closely associated with this institution. It was founded and operated by a private corporation, but with intimate connections to all the Norwegian Lutheran congregations of Brooklyn, including several Synod congregations. Norwegian Lutheran Deaconess Home and Hospital (1897) in Chicago, Illinois, was operated by the Norwegian Lutheran Deaconess Society. It was supported by Synod congregations and members. In a few years the home and hospital were transferred to the United Church. Eventually it was owned (after 1917) by the new merged NLCA. The Norwegian Lutheran Deaconess Institute (1889) in Minneapolis, Minnesota, was supported by Synod congregations and members, but it had been organized by the Conference, and eventually the chief support came from the Lutheran Free Church.

## Miscellaneous Inner Mission Institutions

Two were Synod organized and oriented: the Seamen's Mission (1907) at Seattle, Washington, and the Seamen's Mission (1910) at

Galveston, Texas. Others were independent and carried on by voluntary gifts: Luther Home, a hospice (1904) at Minneapolis, Minnesota, and the Siloah Scandinavian Mission (1907) at Seattle, Washington. In this category, there were other smaller, independent operations. All were Synod-supported. Many of the above charitable and social service institutions became permanent organizations, existing long after the tenure of the Synod ended.

The Synod record in charities and social services was belatedly impressive.

CHAPTER SIXTEEN

# The Union Movement in the Synod

The Synod was deeply involved in union efforts with other Norwegian-American Lutheran groups from its inception. Even before the Synod was fully organized, such efforts were underway. The Synod would remain involved in union negotiations throughout its entire history. This major effort would be a real saga in itself.

In fact, before the Synod was fully constituted, during the organizational period of 1851 through 1853, at the time of its "false start," a real overture was made.

In the summer of 1852, before Pastor H. A. Preus had been in America a whole year, his first confirmation service took place in his Spring Prairie congregation. Preus extended a cordial invitation to Pastor Elling Eielsen of the Eielsen Synod to preach the sermon at that first confirmation service. The Eielsen Synod had been established in 1846, the first Norwegian Lutheran synod on American soil. Thus Preus was reaching out to a sister church body for this special service. Eielsen took advantage of the Spring Prairie pulpit by blasting the Church of Norway and the high church movement in America represented by the emerging Norwegian Synod. He used this special confirmation sermon to take issue with the state church and all its similarities on frontier soil. His sermon was remarkably out-of-order. This event is significant in two ways: First, it was the original ecumenical overture on the part of the Synod. Second, it was the first intentional break and standoff toward the Synod on the part of other Norwegian Lutheran groups or church bodies.

There was almost an immediate attempt to repair the breach—again on Synod initiative. In 1855, when the Synod was just two years old, a conference was held at Spring Prairie between four pastors—two from the Eielsen Synod and two from the Norwegian Synod. (Two of the four were, in fact, Eielsen and Preus.) This attempt did not achieve its desired results, in spite of the earnest effort. The Synod undoubtedly realized at this time that the Eielsen Synod would be a very difficult partner.

In the following decade of the l860s there would be a number of conferences between Synod pastors and other churchmen. Most of these efforts had no immediate results. One of the few tangible results of inter-synodical meetings of this era (l850s and 1860s) was the switch of allegiance on the part of Pastor P. A. Rasmussen. Having left the Eielsen Synod, he joined the Norwegian Synod (1862), where he was destined to become a leader in the union movement and the foreign mission movement.

Most of the inter-synodical conferences in the 1860s were between the Synod and the Norwegian Augustanans, although the Swedish Augustanans were on occasion involved.

## Synod Leadership in Union Activities in the 1870s

*Pan-Lutheran Conference of 1870*

The 1870s began auspiciously. Again the Synod took the lead. The Synod in 1870 attempted to arrange a conference for "all who regard themselves as Lutherans," to be held at Rushford, Minnesota, to explore union possibilities. The invitation was signed by Pastors F. A. Schmidt, A. C. Preus, and J. B. Frich; it was sent out in July. The previous month (June 1870) the Swedish Augustanans and the Norwegian Augustanans had peacefully parted company. This provided the Synod with the hope that the disentangled Norwegian-American Augustanans might be ready to discuss union with the Synod.

However, the disruption of 1870 (away from Synod jurisdiction) had produced the Norwegian-Danish Conference (l870-1890) as well as the Norwegian Augustana Synod (1870-1890). The organizational meeting of the Conference accepted the invitation, but they failed to send any representatives. The Augustanans were busy picking up the pieces of their synodical re-organization at the time the scheduled meeting took place; they did not respond.

Consequently, the Synod leaders found themselves all alone when the "pan-Lutheran" conference convened. Despite this turn of events, the Synod leaders decided to proceed with the meeting and discuss the assigned topic of church unity. This conference/meeting was concluded with the passing of two resolutions: The first resolution expressed the hope that the divisions existing among Norwegian Lutherans might be removed "with the help of God"—and that general conferences would provide the surest means of attaining that objective. The second resolution aimed at reaching the absentees by ordering the printing of the proceedings in the official periodical of the Synod. The minutes of the Rushford Conference of October 11-12, 1870, were published in the Synod's periodical, *Kirkelig Maanedstidende* (1871) in four successive issues.

*General Conferences*

Two general conferences were scheduled at that meeting: the first for June 13-21, 1871, at Decorah, Iowa; the second for 1872 at Rock Prairie (Luther Valley), Wisconsin.

Because the Synod was the only church body at this first conference, they were able to set the agenda for all of the immediate future general conferences on church union. The agenda was very much a leading force, but it was not accepted by all in the other church bodies. The Norwegian-Danish Conference, by accepting and not attending, had no one to blame but themselves; they ran from behind for some time on the church union issue. The Augustanans sidelined themselves by not responding, although in the 1860s, most of the meetings had been between the Synod and the Norwegian-Swedish Augustanans.

The first General (Free) Conference was held at Decorah, June 13-21, 1871. There was a distinct atmosphere of friendliness and willingness to understand each other. The problem of the relationship between Scripture and the Lutheran Confessions received a great deal of attention. Although each side exhibited friendliness and agreed not to consider the expression of an individual member of a church body as the opinion of the whole church body, nevertheless the viewpoints remained basically unchanged from those expressed previously. The editor of *Kirkelig Maanedstidende,* the Synod's official periodical, commented realistically when he said there was more hope for mutual understanding of the doctrines of the gospel and justification than for agreement about the relationship between Scripture and the Confessions.

The second General (Free) Conference was held at Rock Prairie (Luther Valley), Wisconsin, in 1872. The lack of good will and the open hostility which characterized this meeting squashed hopes for immediate progress, and the union movement was virtually at a standstill for a whole decade. The lack of good will was reflected in a strong action. It was at this Rock Prairie Conference that President H. A. Preus issued his "anathema" on the Norwegian-Danish Conference. This anathema would be a thorn in the side of the Conference for the rest of its existence—until 1890. In response to Preus (actually in 1874), Professor Oftedal of the Conference issued his "Public Declaration" (signed also by Professor Weenaas), which rocked the whole church with its immoderate attack on the Synod.

Historians point out that at least the Rock Prairie Conference and the "Public Declaration" served to reveal the points of difference separating the Conference and the Synod. It was clear that little progress toward union could be made until the tension had eased.

Almost a whole decade intervened between conferences—until the 1880s. Still it was the Synod which was setting the agenda for these inter-synod union talks.

## Regional Doctrinal Conferences

In 1877 Synod Pastor B. J. Muus, the founder of St. Olaf's School and the new president of the Synod's Minnesota District, proposed the holding of regional doctrinal conferences. Nine such meetings were held within a year before the Synod's general convention in 1878. These meetings included representatives from Hauge's Synod, the Conference, and the Synod.

Muus reported that, doctrinally speaking, there appeared to be some hope for Hauge's Synod; but, as for the Conference, it was still imprisoned in error. This observation by Muus is highly revealing of his continuing negative attitude toward the Conference. Despite the fact that Muus would be a leader in the Anti-Missourian movement in the 1880s, his essential attitude toward the Conference never changed. From a personal standpoint his attitude was perhaps further accentuated by the fact that his personal interest lay in St. Olaf's School rather than in Augsburg Seminary, which was supported by the Conference.

By 1880 the bitterness between the Synod and the Conference had somewhat abated. In fact, historian J. A. Bergh says that "the internal and external strife of the church bodies opened the eyes of each to their own shortcomings and to the good in the others. By means of this conflict, the ground was broken and prepared for the seeds of peace soon to be sown." In other words, there would be good results.

It was unfortunate that strife had been the result of sincere attempts at union negotiations.

## Synod Leadership in Union Activities in the 1880s

Leadership in union negotiations came in the 1880s from the Synod in the person of Pastor P. A. Rasmussen. Once again the Synod was in the forefront of intersynodical movements and co-operation.

Rasmussen had something of a pan-Lutheran background. He came to America in 1850 as a Haugean layman, was ordained into the Eielsen Synod, joined the Norwegian Synod in 1862, and was one of the Synod's most ardent supporters until the Election Controversy. In 1873 he and Professor F. A. Schmidt represented the Synod at a key meeting of the Norwegian Mission Society (NMS) at Drammen, Norway. In 1879 he called the Synod to account in an article, "What Ails Us?" a comprehensive accounting that could fit almost any church body.

In 1880 Rasmussen issued a proposal for a meeting between the Synod and the Conference for the summer of 1881. The proposal normally would have come before the Synod's general convention, but the Synod was not meeting that year. In 1876 the Synod had divided itself into three districts—Eastern, Iowa, and Minnesota—with annual district conventions and the Synod meeting every third year. Thus his proposal went before the three district conventions instead. The Eastern and Iowa Districts endorsed his plan enthusiastically. However, the Minnesota District not only failed to approve, but pronounced a severe official "judgment" against the Conference, ascribing to it a totally different faith than that which is found in the Word of God and the Lutheran Confessions. This "judgment" stuck for a long time. Thus, even though the approval was two to one in the Synod, it needed to be unanimous district action to become official Synod action.

Rasmussen's plan arrived too late to be considered by the Norwegian-Danish Conference convention, but the official periodical of the Conference commended it highly.

Rasmussen's proposal broke ground for other union developments within the 1880s, but it produced no tangible immediate results. Rasmussen would also be the convener of seven inter-synodical foreign mission meetings 1883-1890, which would aid and abet union activity as well as missions.

*Free Conferences*

Another staunch Synod leader, Pastor B. J. Muus, who was no admirer of the Conference, continued to promote union. In the spring of

1881 Muus persuaded the presidents of the Synod, the Conference, and Hauge's Synod—together with the Synod district presidents of the Minnesota and Iowa Districts and the vice president of the Eastern District—to sign an invitation calling a Free Conference at St. Ansgar, Iowa, June 24-30, 1881. They all signed as individuals, not as representatives of their church bodies or districts.

The first Free Conference of June 24-30, 1881 at St. Ansgar assembled a total of 341 delegates, a good number—164 from the Synod, the largest group, almost a majority; 138 from the Conference; thirty-nine from Hauge's Synod, Norwegian Augustana, Swedish Augustana, and unaffiliated. Seven theses on "Redemption and the Forgiveness of Sins" were discussed. There was a marked spirit of good will throughout this conference and a calculated effort to avoid the controversial issues of the past as much as possible. The controversial issue of "justification of the world" (a Synod concept) came up, but significantly the Synod men stated they would give up this expression because it was so easily misunderstood.

This gathering revealed a very amiable spirit characterized by the willingness to consider others as Lutheran and to engage in full prayer and devotional service fellowship.

The second Free Conference of this decade was held at Roland, Iowa, in October, 1882. There were 165 delegates in attendance: ninety-six from the Synod, a majority; forty from Hauge's Synod; twenty-seven from the Conference; two from the Norwegian Augustana Synod. Five theses were prepared, centering the discussion around faith as the means of appropriating the fruits of Christ's redemption. No serious doctrinal disagreement was evident at Roland.

This conference also passed Professor F. A. Schmidt's recommendation that an official general committee of twenty-eight—seven from each church body—confer on the obstacles to unity and recommend steps toward closer union.

Pastor P. A. Rasmussen urged another free conference to be held in 1883 to discuss the subject of absolution.

The third and last of the Free Conferences of the 1880s was held at Holden Church in Goodhue County, Minnesota, June 27 to July 4, 1883. The discussion on the doctrine of absolution showed that the differences no longer followed synodical lines. The Synod was represented and supported by such leaders as Pastors Muus, Bjorn, Bockman, and Frich, as well as Professors Schmidt, Stub, and Larsen. The opposition was articulated by Professor Weenaas of Augsburg Seminary of the Conference. But there was also a concerted attempt to "harmonize the truths for which both [sides] were striving." As a result, the whole conference was able to subscribe to a set of theses on absolution with almost no opposition raised from any quarter.

The Synod had been a leader in the free conference movement. Synod leaders had been most enthusiastic in promoting free conferences for doctrinal discussion. However, in selecting the subject for the next conference, this conference voted overwhelmingly (125 to 7) in favor of the theme of unity—as opposed to the Synod's proposal for further doctrinal discussions. This revealed a shift to practical church problems and away from doctrinal matters, which had been the traditional agenda.

Further conferences would be "joint meetings," officially approved by the church bodies. A general committee with members elected from each church body would make the arrangements for these "joint (official) meetings." But the free conferences had brought events this far, and the Synod had been a leader in them.

*Three Joint Official Meetings, 1883 to 1887*

A general committee did indeed meet November 14, 1883, at Red Wing, Minnesota. They recommended that a "joint committee" of sixteen members be selected to arrange joint meetings. The joint committee met in October 1884, at Rushford, Minnesota, to arrange for the first joint meeting. Both of the preceding committees had been chosen by the participating church bodies.

The first Joint Meeting took place at Chicago, January 28 to February 5, 1885. Little progress was recorded during prolonged discussion on the topics of redemption and forgiveness. Instead, the main result of the Joint Meeting was the answer given to the question: "What is required in order that the congregations of the four church bodies can recognize one another as Lutheran and be united into one synod?" The answer given was acceptance of the Scriptures and the Lutheran Confessions. It was also specified that the church bodies do not by any official act deny their acceptance of the said scriptures and confessions.

The second Joint Meeting was held in the Gol Church near Kenyon in Goodhue County, Minnesota, May 14-20, 1886. Pastor M. O. Bockman, an anti-Missourian Synod pastor, was the host. The registration was: forty-nine from the Synod (the most), forty-seven from the Conference, and four Norwegian Augustanans. Synod veterans H. A. Preus, U.

V. Koren, and F. A. Schmidt were not present. Neither was anyone from Hauge's Synod, which had discontinued union negotiations.

The committee which had prepared the agenda had suggested a continuation on the subject of mutual recognition of one another as Lutheran synods. But before it considered the proposed agenda, the meeting discussed the practical problems of congregational and foreign mission work. On these practical matters a great deal of progress was made.

The meeting then turned to the agenda and acted to confirm the Chicago (previous) meeting's declaration regarding the Lutheranism of the Symbols (i.e. the Confessions) and draw up a very balanced statement on absolution. The meeting also called upon the Synod's Minnesota District to rescind its "judgment" of 1880 on the Conference. (This was partly achieved the next year.)

Historian E. Clifford Nelson points out that, on the whole, this meeting was another encouragement to those working for union. It was a disappointment that Hauge's Synod was not represented, but New School people of the Conference (in the persons of Professor Sverdrup and Professor Oftedal) were represented. They, pietists like the Haugeans, had previously been unfriendly to the cause.

The third Joint Meeting was held at Willmar, Minnesota, October 6-12, 1887. This meeting took place on Synod territory. Historian Nelson states that in many aspects this was the most important joint meeting. It followed the split in the ranks of the Synod (in June 1887) over the doctrine of election. The question was raised as to whether the Anti-Missourians should be considered as having no synodical affiliation or as a new church body. After much discussion, no synodical affiliation was adopted. (They eventually declared themselves a "brotherhood" instead of a new synod.) From this meeting the Anti-Missourians felt a new identity to promote union and not to add to the fragmentation of the church.

The meeting, by previous arrangement, gave itself to a deliberation of the doctrine of justification. The discussion revealed a large measure of agreement. The subject of justification was introduced by Koren, the Synod's leading theologian. (He was the only one of three designated presenters of different subjects who showed up.) The joint meeting adopted two resolutions which stated that "no church-dividing disunity" existed concerning the doctrines of justification and atonement. No one voted against the two resolutions, although some Synod representatives abstained from voting because they felt the resolutions were incomplete statements of doctrine, a very typical Synod stance and attitude.

The arrangements committee had decided that the Willmar meeting should decide the question: "What hindrances stand in the way of the union movement, and how can they be removed?" The chief obstacles were reported along synodical lines: The Synod looked upon absolution and the intrusion into one another's congregations (parochial comity) as primary. The other church bodies had other issues.

In common with previous joint meetings, the Willmar Joint Meeting unanimously (Synod included) adopted a resolution for a similar meeting the following year. However, despite the agreements reached at Willmar, there was (sadly) no reconciliation within the Synod of the Anti-Missourians and the Synod mainliners. This would lead to the formation of the United Norwegian Lutheran Church in 1890, in which the Anti-Missourian Synod pastors would be the leaders.

Ironically, the Election Controversy within the Synod, and the resulting schism in the Synod, would jump start the union initiatives within the Norwegian-American Lutheran church bodies. The Synod Anti-Missourian pastors, first inside the Synod and then in a new church body, emerged as leaders.

## Union Efforts Between the Synod and the United Norwegian Lutheran Church

Following the formation of the United Church in 1890, the Synod gave expression to continuing interest in the task of gathering all Norwegian-American Lutherans into one church. At the Synod's general convention of 1890, clear and unmistakable statements were drafted showing a concern for the cause of union. The 1889 convention of the Synod's Minnesota District had memorialized the Synod to continue, as far as possible, negotiations with other Norwegian-American Lutheran groups, looking to eventual merger. This memorial was discussed and acted upon positively at the 1890 Synod general convention. The memorial noted that there were disruptive forces at work, but the Synod should consider investing its Union Committee with authority to participate in joint meetings. The convention proceeded to adopt a resolution which embodied the union hopes of the memorial (from the Minnesota District).

The Union Committee had been elected in 1887—right in the middle of the Election Controversy—consisting of Professors Frich and Larsen, and Pastors H. A. Preus, U. V. Koren, Bjug Harstad, and J. A. Thorsen. Now in 1890 they added two more names: Professors Stub and Ylvisaker. This was a committee of eight prominent members.

Later that year (1890) there was a private (personal invitation) colloquy in Minneapolis, meeting December 29-31. Present were professors from Luther Seminary (Synod), Augsburg Seminary (United), and St. Olaf College. A common agreement was reached that all must consider one another as Lutherans.

One of the results of the 1890 Synod Convention, and especially its resolution regarding union, was the initiation of union negotiations with the brand new United Church. The United Church, too, at its constituting 1890 convention had elected a committee of five members to discuss possible union with the Synod. The two committees met in Madison, April 7-8, 1891. It was decided at this meeting that each church body elect thirty representatives to confer on the issue of union. Hauge's Synod was also invited, but the meeting would still go forward it they did not accept.

The joint committee suggested this topic for the proposed meeting: "What are the requisites of church union?" They also suggested a second area of discussion devoted to absolution or conversion. (Apparently, doctrinal discussion still needed to be a part of every meeting.)

The first major meeting of the union committees was held at Willmar, Minnesota, January 6-12, 1892. Only the Synod and the United Church were present; Hauge's Synod had not accepted the invitation. It does not appear that the joint committee's suggested agenda was followed. Instead, the meeting revealed different points of view on ecclesiastical and doctrinal matters which had not been thoroughly discussed at previous inter-synodical conferences—primarily the question of prayer fellowship and the inspiration of the scriptures.

Much of the discussion was on the second question; namely, the inspiration of the scriptures. All sides agreed on inspiration, although some Synod representatives promoted defining the mode of inspiration (i.e. verbal inspiration). A committee was chosen to draw a resolution on which all could agree. The committee presented the following:

> In regard to church union between the Synod and the United Church we consider the unanimous acceptance of the canonical books of the Holy Scriptures as God's revealed, infallible Word on the part of both church bodies as a fully sufficient

basis for church union. Note: Our position in relation to Holy Scripture is given expression in Pontoppidan's answers to Questions 12, 15, and 18 in *Sandhed Til Gudfrygtighed—Truth Unto Godliness.*"

The resolution was unanimously adopted as the expression of the conference.

The conference did reveal that the two groups, which had taken opposite positions on other issues, now were taking differing views on prayer fellowship, inspiration, and the place of the Book of Concord. Historian E. Clifford Nelson points out that problems raised at this conference would continue as issues within American Lutheranism through most of the twentieth century.

Nelson also states that, in fairness to both parties, there was essential agreement on all three issues: On prayer fellowship it was the feeling of all (including most of the Synod, which sometimes had raised this issue) that it was not right to deny corporate prayer. Regarding inspiration, both sides were agreed that the Bible is the Word of God, though they differed on the question of whether the theory (the mode) of inspiration be made a condition of union. Both groups looked upon the Book of Concord as a correct exposition of Lutheran doctrine, but there was disagreement as to whether the largely unknown documents—such as the Apology of the Augsburg Confession, the Smalcald Articles, and the Formula of Concord—ought to be placed on the churches as required Lutheran Confessions. (The Synod may have been supporting the inclusion of the lesser-known documents, even though these documents had not been a part of the Danish-Norwegian heritage of both groups.)

The delegates at Willmar recognized that the time for union had not yet come, and so they made no provisions for similar meetings in the future. There were two realities that stood in the way: First, the breach between the Synod mainliners and the Anti-Missourians was still too recent and raw. The wounds of that conflict had not yet healed. Second, the United Church was engaged in an internal struggle of its own, which caused many to take a dim view of new attempts at union. The Augsburg Controversy was moving toward its climax. Consequently, five years were to elapse before the calling of another major free conference.

The second major meeting, a free conference, was held at Lanesboro, Minnesota, September 15-22, 1897. In the late summer of 1897, Synod Pastor B. J. Muus took the initiative in reviving interest in the resumption of inter-church negotiations. Basically this was a Synod initiative. Muus was technically a Synod man.

Obtaining the signatures of sixty-nine pastors of the three church bodies (Synod, United Church, Hauge's Synod) Muus issued an invitation to a major free conference to be held at Lanesboro, Minnesota, September 15-22, 1897. The subject for discussion was the doctrine of conversion, which was a Muus favorite. It quickly led the conferees back to the Election Controversy of the 1880s, in which the question was asked: "What, if any, is man's part in conversion?" How to ascribe salvation solely to God (the main-line Synod emphasis) and not detract from man as a responsible personality (the Anti-Missourian emphasis) was the nub of the problem. The discussion went back and forth for a whole week. Neither side was ready to admit the other side possessed insight into the truth. In fact, the mainline Synod and Anti-Missourian sides stood out more sharply than ever before.

Nelson states that the significance of this meeting lay in the fact that substantially the same positions would be maintained uncompromisingly for the next thirteen years. Although the stalemate would not be fully recognized until 1910, it had already been reached in 1897.

A resolution was adopted to continue the discussion at a subsequent major free conference. A committee, including Stub of the Synod, was charged with arrangements.

The third major free conference was held at Austin, Minnesota, January 18-15, 1899—which was just sixteen months later.
This conference was marked by poor attendance; there were only forty-four participants. Only one Synod participant showed up. He was Pastor Rasmus Malmin, who was to become one of the most active participants in the inter-church negotiations leading up to the Settlement of 1912.

The discussion at Austin continued the agenda of the Lanesboro Conference on conversion. The deliberations centered around a set of theses by Professor F. A. Schmidt. As expected, the debate led nowhere. This conference probably did not contribute negatively or positively to union negotiations. Its significance lay in the fact that it sounded the death-knell of the large major free conferences.

A discussion meeting took place in 1900 at Thor, Iowa. Local in nature, this meeting nevertheless brought together Synod representatives and representatives from the United Church. Synod and United Church representatives were willing to convene and discuss the issues. The debate on election revealed the traditional differences between the two sides.

## The Twentieth Century

Historian Nelson points out that the years 1900-1912 are, in some respects, the most important in the history of the union movement among Norwegian-American Lutherans. During these years divisive procedural and doctrinal problems, which had plagued the church for decades, were settled. Opposite tendencies which had existed in the church since pioneer days lost some of their sharpness. And men of differing viewpoints began to draw closer together.

The Synod began this period with a special initiative, a meeting of interest in union at Luther Seminary, March 28-30, 1901. In 1900 the Synod determined to show that it had not given up the hope of reaching an understanding with the other Norwegian Lutherans in America. Therefore, in convention, the Synod adopted resolutions deploring the existing ecclesiastical divisions and inviting the presidents and theological faculties of the United Church and Hauge's Synod to a colloquy on doctrine.

Only the United Church accepted the invitation, The meeting took place at the Synod's Luther Seminary just before Easter, March 28-30, 1901. The church body presidents and professors gave evidence of reaching a common view of the assurance of salvation, based on some discussion theses. These theses were presented by the United Church's President Gjermund Hoyme. The assembled group adopted a resolution to continue the discussion the following year.

Unfortunately, a severe setback and roadblock came from within the United Church in the person of Professor F. A. Schmidt, one of the participants. Before the next meeting, Schmidt published a partial account of the colloquy's proceedings. This was absolutely contrary to the wish of the colloquy. It was a broken commitment. And because Schmidt went out of his way to describe Hoyme's theses as a "compromise to bridge the chasm between truth and error," the Synod took proper exception. The Synod passed a resolution in 1902 requesting the United Church to replace Schmidt in the joint discussion with another man who was to be less likely to be "a hindrance" to the cause of union. This the United Church refused to do. In the process the Synod charged Schmidt with incorrigibility. His action would be a sticking-point in union negotiations for several years to follow.

Instead of cooperating, the United Church elected a committee to answer the charge against Schmidt. The committee's reply took pains to answer each charge of the Synod and concluded by accusing the Synod of defaming Schmidt. The reply urged the Synod to confess its "great sins." This was an abrasive reply by the United Church.

All of this could have been avoided if the agreed-upon procedures had been followed. It appears that the Synod was basically in order. But the Synod did take exception to the United Church action. The decade was off to a rough start.

The United Church called an unofficial free conference for 1903. Both the Synod and Hauge's Synod declined the invitation to participate. Union interest apparently reached its lowest point from 1903 to 1905.

In 1905 the United Church adopted a despairing resolution instructing its church president and seminary faculty to do "what they could" to promote union. It seemed to be an effort without hope. But very co-incidentally Hauge's Synod, meeting at the same time, announced that they had elected a committee to consider union "with other Norwegian Lutheran synods." This was the turning point in union negotiations; it is what the others had been waiting for.

Hauge's Synod had previously withdrawn from union activities for about fifteen years, from 1890 to 1905. Now Hauge's Synod called for its brand-new union committee to meet with similar committees. The Hauge's Synod Convention dispatched telegrams to the Synod Convention and the United Church Convention, both of which were meeting simultaneously, and requested each to appoint a union committee. Both bodies immediately complied, in convention assembled.

The result was that there would be three joint union committee meetings the next year, in 1906.

*Three Joint Union Committee Meetings 1906*

The first two Joint Union Committee meetings were held in Minneapolis on January 17 and from March 27 to 31. Both were conducted in a spirit of friendliness and genuine good will. Both meetings were opened and closed with common prayer.

The major achievement of these first two meetings was agreement on the doctrine of absolution. Five theses covering the various aspects of the controversy, which had been carried on among the church bodies since 1861, were unanimously adopted at these meetings. The report was signed by Brandt (Synod), Eastvold (Hauge's Synod), and Johnsen (United Church); it bore the date March 30, 1906. The report was presented to the annual conventions of the three bodies that year. (An English translation of this report is found in the *Union Documents of the Evangelical Lutheran Church*, page 28.) This action was all-important. Historians point out that these propositions on absolution were virtually identical to those adopted by the Synod in 1874, which was thirty-two years before. These theses, previously prepared by Professor Schmidt (then a member of the Synod), were now objected to by Schmidt. President Stub (in 1911) points out that the 1906 meetings were largely the answering of Schmidt's arguments against his own theses, which he had forgotten were his.

The third meeting of the Joint Union Committee of 1906 took place in Minneapolis October 16-19. This meeting resulted in agreement on the troublesome problem of lay activity in the church. The document covering this subject was called "Lay Ministries in the Church." It was signed by the same representatives of the respective union committees. An English translation is in the *Union Documents*, pages 28-30. The significant feature of this document is that it was able to state the attitude of the churches on this subject in such a way that satisfied the Synod, which had serious reservations about lay ministries in the church and guaranteed to Hauge's Synod the essential preservation of this aspect of the Haugean tradition in America.

It should be noted that lay activity was definitely regulated; that regulation was maintained by placing the emphasis not on ordination, but on the call and supervision by the church. This was the solution to this long-time, troublesome question which had plagued inter-synodical relationships.

The fourth meeting of the Joint Union Committee took place in Minneapolis, March 19-22, 1907. There would be two extensions to this fourth meeting: A second conference would be in October 1907 and third conference would follow in April 1908.

It had been decided at the previous meeting to consider the doctrines of the call and conversion at this fourth meeting. According to the previous agreement, a separate synodical committees would prepare an introduction respectively on each subjects. Both preparations would be made on the bases of Pontoppidan's *Truth Unto Godliness*, the catechism explanation with which both groups were very familiar. The United Church committee was to introduce the call on the basis of question #478. The

Synod committee was to introduce conversion on the basis of question #677. The discussions took longer than expected, and therefore the two meeting extensions were added.. It was at the third and last conference of this meetig that agreement was reached on the doctrines of the call and conversion. And the Joint Committee reported a unanimous acceptance of all the theses that pertained and had been discussed.

The doctrinal agreement on the call contained six theses. The statement on conversion was more lengthy and detailed, containing eleven paragraphs. The English translation for both sets of theses is in *The Union Documents*, pages 31-38. In 1911 President Stub commented on the results of this extended meeting, that not since the Election Controversy had the Synod and United Church stood so close.

An addendum to this Joint Union Committee report had this meaningful statement: "Dr. Schmidt requested it be added to the minutes that he did not take part in the voting on paragraph eleven ('. . . the glory belongs to God alone . . .'); neither was Dr. Schmidt present at the last meeting when paragraphs 6b and c on the call were adopted." Apparently Professor Schmidt, the old leader of the Anti-Missourians in the Election Controversy, found the hard-hitting phrases of the paragraphs too much; he had fought to establish the place of man in conversion.

*The Synod Convention*

President U. V. Koren of the Synod surprisingly made no reference to the relevant work of the Joint Union Committee in his annual report to the Synod Convention in 1908. However, a formal and conventionally phrased and strong resolution expressing gratitude and joy over progress in inter-synodical relations was adopted by the Synod in convention assembled, with 225 ayes, five nays, and twenty-one abstentions, for a total of 251 votes. The result was 89.6 percent, or almost 90 percent, had voted approval. This indicates overwhelming Synod support for the results of the union movement. Interestingly, Pastor Bjug Harstad, who later became a leader in the opposition to union, requested that his name be entered in the minutes as abstaining from voting. The other two church bodies also voted approval--Hauge's Synod somewhat reluctantly, the United Church overwhelmingly and enthusiastically.

*Joint Union Committee Meetings*

By 1908 a number of forces had come together to press for union. The success of the years 1905-1908 via the Joint Union Committee had contributed to this momentum. However, that success was to receive a serious setback and real difficulties when the Joint Union Committee faced the troublesome doctrine of election. During 1908 through 1910, the essential disagreement over election flared up again. Election was to be the subject of discussion at the next joint meeting of the union committees, scheduled for later that same year, November 10-13, in Minneapolis. The Synod took an active part in the Joint Union Committee negotiations to resolve the disagreements over the doctrine of election.

The first Joint Union Committee meeting took place April 7, 1908, at Our Savior's Church in Minneapolis. This meeting, which resolved the doctrines of the call and conversion, also set the agenda for the next Joint Union Committee meeting in November 1908. It also named a sub-committee to prepare theses for this forthcoming meeting.

The second meeting of the Joint Union Committee took place on November 10-13, 1908, in Minneapolis. It fruitlessly debated Professor Stub's theses. Note that the Synod took the initiative by submitting the basis for discussion.

The third meeting, March 30 to April 2, 1909, served only to reveal more clearly the bipolarity of the mainline Synod and anti-Missourian positions on election. The Fourth Meeting, November 2-5, 1909, ground to a halt over election. It then referred the subject to a sub-committee to prepare a new statement for discussion. The sub-committee was unable to reach an agreement.

The fifth meeting took place on March 10, 1910. This would become a very difficult meeting. Dr. Stub, who had just become the president of the Synod, was apparently also the chairman of the Joint Union Committee. In spite of the fact that the sub-committee had been unable in the interim (November 1909 to March 1910) to reach an agreement on a new statement for discussion, Chairman Stub found it advisable to convene the whole Joint Committee on the previously established conditional date, although agreement in the sub-committee had been the condition upon which Dr. Stub was to call the whole committee together. In the interim Dr. Stub showed extra initiative by revising his theses, which had been the subject of discussion at the three previous meetings. Dr. Bockman of the United Church then presented a revised edition of the theses which he had earlier submitted. Finally, a new set of theses, prepared by Hauge's Synod's President C. J. Eastvold, was placed before the conference.

The Joint Union Committee then acted to approve the action of Dr. Stub in calling the meeting and to make President Eastvold's theses the basis for discussion. When Eastvold's theses were adopted as the basis for discussion, the Synod representatives objected and submitted the following declaration: "The committee elected by the Norwegian Synod for doctrinal negotiations with committees from the United Church and Hauge's Synod abides by the resolution adopted at the November meeting of the committee: 'If the so-called subcommittee is unable to present a joint declaration, the joint committee will not meet for further negotiations.' In the meantime, the committee will report back to the Synod and await its decision as to whether it will still urge continuation of these meetings in view of the prolonged discussions concerning election and the assurance of salvation." It appears, sadly, that the Synod representatives were caught in a situation of self-contradiction.

At this point the representatives of the Synod left the meeting. Those remaining began a discussion of Eastvold's theses. Since this was obviously a waste of time, the Joint Committee voted to adjourn. Before doing so, however, it was decided to publish the proceedings of the last two years regarding the proceedings dealing with election. This was to be the report of the Joint Committee to the annual conventions of the three participating church bodies.

The official reports to the church bodies omitted an important resolution, however, which showed that union efforts would not be dropped: "Resolved, that we rescind the resolution in regard to discontinuing negotiations on doctrine." Thus it appeared that union efforts were at a standstill in 1910, but in reality they were not.

The Synod held district conventions in 1910. Neither the synod president nor the five district presidents made any reference in their annual reports to the question of union. Nevertheless, resolutions containing interest in the cause of union were presented to each of the five districts. One of the district resolutions—from the Eastern District—declared that the doctrine of election in two forms should not be regarded as schismatic. This action turned out to be a springboard for the union committees to believe that further negotiations would be fruitful.

Based on that resolution, another meeting of the Joint Union Committee, its sixth, was held at the United Church Seminary in St. Paul, December 13-14, 1910. The subject was election. Dr. Stub, the Synod president as well as chairman of the Joint Union Committee, read a statement to the group: It expressed the position of the Synod as that of adherence to Article XI of the Formula of Concord (the so-called first form) as the correct form of the Lutheran doctrine of election. However, the Synod did not consider the use of second form (*intuitu fidei* or question #548 of Pontoppidan) as a cause for division. This should have been the long-awaited break-through which would solve the long-standing inter-synodical problem. This fact needed to be the basis for all discussions and consideration which followed.

Stub mentioned that the Synod's five districts had decided to continue negotiations. But Stub went on to say more: Since the decision of the Synod districts to continue discussions, it had been learned that something had happened in the 1910 general convention of the United Church; namely, President Dahl in his presidential message had charged that the Synod theses (which were Stub's) were unbiblical and un-Lutheran. (It is noteworthy that President Dahl's statement was not on the table with whom it counted; namely, the other members of the Joint Union Committee.) Stub continued that had the Synod known of this earlier, the Synod would hardly have agreed to continue negotiations.

This action by the United Church president was certainly out of order and hostile toward the Synod. It did not facilitate negotiations, in spite of the fact that the United Church claimed they were promoting such negotiations.

Sadly, the Synod responded a little bit in kind. In view of this, Stub continued, the Synod representatives would make their continued participation in the joint meeting contingent upon presentation by the United Church of proof that the Synod position was in error, and that these proofs be made the basis for further deliberations. The Synod should have been forgiving. At the very least, they could have requested clarification in a most friendly and non-challenging manner. There was no percentage in perpetuating whatever bad-blood had existed between these two church bodies.

But the hostile atmosphere continued. The tenor of the meeting was evident from the motion made by Professor E. K. Johnson of the United Church in which, with complete disregard for Stub's statement, he urged that President Eastvold's theses be made the basis for deliberation.
When this motion was adopted, Stub understandably announced that the Synod representatives would not participate in the discussion.

More back-and-forth conversation followed. The United Church committee reminded the Synod that at a previous meeting, when the Joint Committee decided in favor of Stub's theses as over against Kildahl's, the

United Church committee did not leave the meeting in a huff. The United Church union committee continued: Now, however, when a discussion was proposed over statements prepared by one (Eastvold) who had not been a party to the earlier election strife, it was only fair that the Synod acquiesce to the majority. To this Stub replied that at the earlier meeting it was a question of form; now it was a matter of conscience.

An attempt to reach a compromise by suggesting that the United Church representatives present one or more points of difference for discussion the next day proved ineffective. The session ended with the Synod delegation withdrawing from further negotiations.

The next day, December 14, the two remaining committees discussed, came to an agreement on election, and declared themselves ready for union. They also went on record as deploring the withdrawal of the Synod committee.

## *The Interim Year of 1911*

Following the March 1910 and December 1910 joint meetings of the union committees, discussion on the disputed subject, election, came to an impasse. Progress seemed impossible—in fact, out of the question. During 1911 there were skirmishes primarily between Stub, speaking for the Synod, and Professor J. N. Kildahl of the United Church.

It is important to point out that the United Church president, T. H. Dahl, had publicly declared (with no direct consultation) Stub's theses on election to be unbiblical and un-Lutheran, and that this charge had been the cause for the walkout of the Synod delegates. Kildahl responded by saying the essential reason for the present deadlock was the "adamant attitude" of the Norwegian Synod. The Synod committee, while defending its position, expressed real sorrow over the stalemate: "We express our profound regrets, that a task which has so long commanded our best efforts, and for the successful consummation of which we entertained such splendid hopes, should terminate here. We had in all sincerity believed that the United Church men had approached more closely to us."

Then, in March 1911, President Stub wrote in the Synod's official organ a defense of his theses. He went back to the first meeting between the Synod and the United Church in 1901 at Luther Seminary. He referred to the actions and words of Professor Schmidt as being chiefly responsible for the present bind. Moreover, the fact that the United Church committee refused to disavow Schmidt served only to aggravate the situation.

The document prepared by the union committee of the United Church was essentially a defense of President Dahl's statement at the United Church convention in 1910, which stated that Stub's theses could not be considered biblical and Lutheran. (The United Church never did take back this statement, and this fact served really to hold up union negotiations.) An addendum to this report, however, did express its willingness to discuss doctrine further.

These two writings served only to entrench each side in its firmly established position; namely, the charge of "Calvinism" against the mainline Synod position and "synergism" against the Anti-Missourian position. Neither side would budge.

Historian Nelson advances three possible reasons for the impasse of 1911. The first is the illusive and hardly accessible factor of personalities. Personality conflicts are hard to measure. Two items should be noted. First, Stub and Kildahl had been involved in the 1880s Election Controversy, and now in 1908-1911 they were chief protagonists. It would be hard for them and others who had been involved previously to forget the conflicts of fifteen to twenty years earlier. Second, F. A. Schmidt continued to serve on the Joint Union Committee. His untoward actions in 1901 exacerbated the Synod's resistance to continuing conversation, and his conduct throughout the decade had made his presence doubly *persona non grata* in the union meetings.

The second factor in the deadlock of 1911 was the failure to recognize that there had been some changes in the intervening years. Nelson says that "the evidence points out that the United Church was the chief offender in failing to note this." Previously, the counter-charges of "synergism" and "Calvinism" had flown rather freely. However, in the first decade of the twentieth century there had been a noticeable change among the Synod representatives, especially the new president, H. G. Stub. The bogeyman of synergism was less frequently invoked by them. And, although they retained the first form viewpoint of the *Formula of Concord*, by and large they acknowledged that the second form of the doctrine of election ought not to be considered divisive for church unity.

It is even worth noting that in 1884 the Synod's document, *An Accounting*, (written by Koren and sent to the congregations)—right in the middle of the Election Controversy—had reluctantly conceded the second form as being non-heretical though incomplete and thus dangerous. Unfortunately, Professor F. A. Schmidt of the United Church continued to accuse the Synod of Calvinism at every turn. Schmidt simply could not forget that he was no longer back in the nineteenth century. On occasion, he acted as though he were still fighting Professor Walther of the Missouri Synod. It must be admitted that the presence of Schmidt on the Joint Union Committee and the hesitation of his colleagues to silence him or to apologize for his occasional inexcusable outbursts played no little part in the cooling of union interest among leaders of the Synod.

The third factor in the 1911 standoff was the opposite theological methods of the two groups. Historian Nelson terms it "Antithetical Theological Method." The two theological emphases had not yet been reconciled: The Synod approached the doctrine of election from the viewpoint of God's decree in eternity. The United Church approached the same doctrine of election from the viewpoint of the actualization of God's decree in time.

*The Breakthrough Madison Agreement of 1912*

The general view of union in 1911 was hopeless. However, historians point out that three significant issues continued to point the Synod toward union.

First, the attitudes of three key Synod leaders—President H.G. Stub, Dr. Laur. Larsen, Luther College president emeritus and current Synod periodical editor, and Pastor Rasmus Malmin—changed.

The second initiative was a common hymnal and service book. Again the Synod showed the initiative. The Synod committee for preparing an English hymnbook approached the United Church committee in 1908 about possible cooperation on the new project. The two committees began working together and continued throughout the period of doctrinal discussion. The result in 1913 was *The Lutheran Hymnary*, which served the separate and later combined church bodies for over forty-five years, until a new hymnal was published in 1958.

The third issue pointing forward was the attitude of the laity in all branches of the three church bodies. The laity basically and almost unanimously wanted union—and made it known at every turn and opportunity.

In 1911 both the Synod and the United Church held their regular general conventions in St. Paul. Both elected new union committees, consisting entirely of parish pastors. Both church bodies seemed to sense that professors, synodical presidents, and church officials had not been able to get over the old issues of the doctrine of election. They now charged new union committees of parish pastors with the task.

Because the United Church convention met first, they chose to send a fraternal delegate (instead of the usual formal greeting) to the Synod convention. The Synod welcomed the delegate and his warm greeting. President Stub responded by graciously accepting the greeting. But Stub also reminded his convention and the fraternal delegate that the United Church had branded the Synod unbiblical and un-Lutheran. This was a sticking-point. And the United Church never retracted this accusation. But President Stub continued that we ". . . have always been and even now are willing to carry on negotiations with them."

The new Joint Union Committee met in St. Paul at the YMCA later that year, in November 1911. Hauge's Synod decided to remain outside these negotiations—leaving the deliberations up to the two committees, instead of three. Both groups went out of their way to be friends with the other. The Synod committee invited the United Church committee to lunch. The United Church committee planned that each of their members would befriend a specific member of the Synod committee.
In this way they both hoped to begin and operate in an amiable fashion and to overcome personality conflicts from the start. It was a good beginning.

This first meeting did serve the purpose of acquainting members with each other. When it became apparent that the Joint Committee as a whole could not reach a common theological understanding, they chose a sub-committee to draft proposals. When the sub-committee indicated they needed more time, they were made a permanent subcommittee. The Joint Committee meeting was then scheduled for later. Synod Pastor Rasmus Malmin was chosen as chairman of the four-member subcommittee.

The subcommittee met at the West Hotel in Minneapolis during the next month, December 1911. Members of the joint committee were requested to present proposals to the subcommittee in writing. The suggestions were considered, and after thorough deliberation, agreement was reached in the subcommittee. A document embracing the consensus of the four men was prepared.

The second Joint Union Committee neeting was convened February 14, 1912, at the Park Hotel in Madison, Wisconsin. They in effect went into seclusion at the hotel for nine days. Naturally, the subcommittee's report was the chief item of business. However, upon the suggestion of Pastor Malmin, the subcommittee chairman, the joint committee first of all turned to a discussion of the doctrine of election as presented in the *Formula of Concord*, Article XI (the so-called first form). This study occupied the joint committee for five days. On February 19 the joint committee turned to the so-called second form of the doctrine of election, question #548 in Pontoppidan's *Truth Unto Godliness*.

When this discussion was completed, the joint committee turned to the report of the subcommittee. The first point in the proposal read as follows: "The union committees of the Synod and the United Church, unanimously and without reservation, accept that doctrine of election which is set forth in the *Formula of Concord*, Part II, Article XI and in Pontoppidan's *Truth Unto Godliness*, question #548." It was decided that the following two parenthetical phrases be added: after Article XI, "the so-called First Form;" and after question #548, "the so-called Second Form."

The next item of the subcommittee report (which was a statement on the relation between the two forms) encountered some disagreement, whereupon the resolution was placed in the hands of a subcommittee of two. When this more lengthy statement was read, the entire resolution was adopted by a rising unanimous vote. This led the Joint Union Committee to declare "that the essential agreement concerning these doctrines which has been attained is sufficient for church union." The report took pains to avoid all possible avenues for the entrance of synergism (four safeguards) and all theological pitfalls of Calvinism (five safeguards).

On February 22, 1912, the report from the Joint Union Committee of the Synod and the United Church "was completed and unanimously recommended to the churches." This concluded the immediate (1908-1912) challenges facing the union committees on resolving the doctrine of election. Actually, it concluded over forty years of Norwegian-American Lutheran strife over this troublesome doctrine. For the vast majority in the Synod and in the other two church bodies, the way was now paved to Norwegian-American Lutheran unity, which was still five years away.

It has been reported that this Madison Agreement of 1912 was best described as a victory of heart over head. It was an instrument of ecclesiastical rapproachment rather than an astute and flawless display of theological finality with regard to the doctrine of election. Basically, it stated that both first and second forms were acceptable. Every member could pick their own form, and they could not be condemned or excluded by another for their choices. There remained just one Lutheran doctrine of election, but in two forms.

## The Actual Grand Union of 1917

The Synod played a major role in the achievement of the Grand Union of Norwegian-American Lutheran church bodies, following the Madison Agreement of 1912.

The Synod's reaction to the Madison Agreement of 1912 was spontaneous and jubilant. All across the Upper Midwest both congregations and the secular press reacted favorably. Congregations celebrated the action, and church bells rang in recognition.

The only exception was the editorial response of the *Lutheran Herald*, the new English organ of the Synod. A restrained and noncommittal attitude in the early weeks gave way to open questioning and unqualified advice to proceed slowly. The explanation of this editorial response lies in the fact that the editor was Pastor Theodore Graebner of the Missouri Synod. Pastor Graebner had been "on loan" to the Norwegian Synod; in that capacity he had served the Synod as pastor and teacher at Red Wing, Minnesota, from 1900 to 1906 and as home/city missionary in the Chicago area from 1906 to 1908. In 1912 he was again serving a Missouri Synod congregation in Chicago. But the Synod had retained him as editor of the new *Lutheran Herald* on the side. The next year (1913) Graebner would join the faculty of Concordia Seminary in St. Louis, where he would serve for thirty-seven years. Thus the editorial position of the *Lutheran Herald* was really Missouri Synod input.

Despite this, however, the general elation over the Madison Agreement gave indication that the Synod (and the other church bodies) would take favorable action on the reports of the Joint Union Committee in the spring/summer of 1912.

In 1912 the Synod met in district conventions only. All five districts unanimously approved the previous reports on absolution, lay activity, the call, and conversion. But the Madison Agreement ran into some trouble. The main opposition was directed against the doctrinal settlement of election in two forms.

President Stub, anticipating difficulties, had prepared his annual report with the utmost care and sought to allay the fears of those who were dubious about the Settlement. He emphasized that the Settlement was the acceptance not of the two forms, but of the one doctrine expressed in the two forms, and that every member was to use the form which their individual conviction dictated, without any strictures on fellowship or recognition of any other person holding to the other form as a good Lutheran.

The Minnesota District met first (May 30—June 5) at Willmar, Minnesota, and set the pattern for the other districts. The convention approved the Settlement by a unanimous vote of 209. The non-voting advisory members approved it nineteen to one. When all the districts had met, 591 voting members and sixty-seven advisory members approved; fifteen negative votes were cast; twenty abstained from voting. The results were over-whelming: There was 94 percent approval overall with abstentions, and 97 percent approval when excluding the abstentions. The Madison Agreement was further supported by the decision of all the districts to continue committee negotiations with the United Church and Hauge's Synod.

*Union Committee Negotiations after the Madison Agreement*

Each church body appointed a new union committee following the Madison Agreement. The three newly-appointed committees would meet as a Joint Union Committee on September 4-5, 1912.

However, before that meeting President Stub felt compelled to attend the Synodical Conference convention in August 1912, at Saginaw, Michigan. Stub invited his seminary colleague, Professor Johannes Ylvisaker, to come with him. They attended this meeting to defend the Madison Agreement from attacks being made upon it by the Synod's (and Stub's) German friends in the Missouri Synod. Many pastors in the Synod were strongly influenced by the attitude of Missouri Synod theologians; and this was now causing some division of feeling within the Synod.

The results of this trip were not very positive. The Synodical Conference waited until Stub and Ylvisaker had left town to draw their reply, titled "An Appeal to the Synod." They requested three major counter-actions to the Madison Agreement from the Synod. In evaluation, they were sneaky and uncordial in their response; they should have been open and on the table, as Stub had been with them in the Synodical Conference convention.

Moreover, this meeting led to attacks on Stub and the Synod by such Missouri Synod publications as *The Lutheran Witness*, *Der Lutheraner*, and *Lehre und Wehre*, as well as attacks by the Wisconsin Synod in *Theologische Quartaschrift*. In addition, and maybe most important, a book on the subject was written by Professor Franz Pieper of Concordia Seminary titled (in translation) *Conversion and Election: A Plea of a United Lutheranism in America*. Synod Pastor G. T. Lee reviewed this book, commending certain portions, but severely criticizing it for rank injustice to the second form understanding of election.

During the rest of 1912 and into 1913 Stub felt many of these written attacks were unjust. He became aware of other acute attacks on the Synod for having given the Madison Agreement overwhelming approval in the district conventions of 1912. Stub considered these outside attacks to be an open declaration of war; and he submitted the whole matter to the Synod's church council, which supported him. He prepared protests to the Synodical Conference and to the editor of *Lehre und Wehre*.

Despite Stub's detailed defense of the Madison Agreement, and evidence that the Synod on the whole stood behind him, it became clear that a very belligerently articulate minority had developed within the Synod, most clearly seen in the articles and editorials now appearing in the *Lutheran Herald*.

Then there appeared an anonymous and secret document known as "The Petition" (*Bonskrift*). It was circulated among selected pastors of the Synod; it sought to thwart union with the United Church until complete unity in faith (i.e. agreement) had been obtained, and to that end it solicited support. This document was sent only to those who were sympathetic to its declarations. Naturally, President Stub was not on the mailing list, but not surprisingly a copy came into his hands. Upon reading it, Stub and Dr. Laur. Larsen published a "Warning" in the Synod's Norwegian periodical, *Evangelisk-Lutherk Kirketidende*, testifying against its anonymity and factional character.

The result was that the authors revealed their identity by publishing it over their signatures, without commentary or explanation, in *Evangelisk-Lutherk Kirketidende*. The drafters of the document turned out to be none other than Stub's three theological colleagues on the seminary faculty: Professors O. E. Brandt, Johannes Ylvisaker, and Elling Hove. The three professors, who were otherwise great men, were very embarrassed to have their identity revealed and their unethical conduct exposed.

To deal with all this, at the call of the church council, in June 1913, the Synod met in extraordinary convention because of the seriousness of the union question. A synodical general convention ordinarily would not have been held until 1914. This convention would witness a majority and minority report from its union committees. The majority report was drafted by a joint meeting of the Synod's Union Committees of 1911 and 1912 respectively. Its report empowered the Synod Union Committee to work toward an organic union of the three church bodies. On the other hand, the minority report stressed that the unsettled doctrinal questions had to be clarified before the Union Committee could be authorized to negotiate a merger.

Dr. Stub himself was the chief spokesman for the majority in two addresses. In the first he directly answered "The Petition," charging the authors with perpetrating an irresponsible act, indicating that both the manner and intent of "The Petition" would serve only to harm mutual confidence and further the party spirit in the church. In the second address he pleaded for overwhelming approval of the majority report, stating that not to do so would be to break faith with Hauge's Synod and the United Church.

The vote for approval was overwhelming with 78.8 percent favoring the majority report and 21.2 percent favoring the minority report. The actual vote was 394 for the majority report and 106 for the minority report, with a total of 500 convention delegate votes cast.

In spite of the favorable vote, the whole matter was submitted to the congregations of the Synod for final approval. The results of the congregational referendum were announced a year later at the 1914 regular Synod general convention, and they were even more overwhelming: 359 congregations in favor (93 percent), twenty-seven congregations opposed (7 percent).

At the 1914 general convention, Stub ruled: "According to the constitution of the Synod, all congregations which did not vote within the time limits set by the constitution are regarded as having endorsed the resolution of the body." This made the result even more overwhelming: 359 congregations in favor plus 243 not voting equaled 602 recorded in favor, or 95.7 percent, with twenty-seven congregations opposed, or 4.3 percent. There were 629 congregations in the Synod according to the 1913 parochial report.

Supported by this strong synodical majority and the overwhelming congregational approval, the Union Committee of the Synod was now prepared to continue merger negotiations with the Hauge's Synod and United Church union committees.

*The Synod Minority in Autumn 1913*

The overwhelming action at the 1913 extraordinary convention of the Synod did not cause the minority opposition to subside. If anything, it became more vocal by soliciting and obtaining encouragement from the Missouri Synod.

The leaders who emerged from the Synod-wide minority were President C. K. Preus of Luther College, who was also vice president of the Synod during its last six years (1911-1917), and Pastor I. B. Torrison of First Lutheran Church, Decorah, Iowa.

Meanwhile, Dr. Stub made every effort to pacify the minority and to win their support for the cause of union.

Dr. Laur. Larsen, president emeritus of Luther College and until 1912 editor of the Synod's Norwegian organ, *Evangelisk-Lutherk Kirketidende*, emerged as an aid to President Stub in support of the cause of union. In his last years he devoted himself fully to promoting this effort. Convinced that the danger to true Lutheranism in America had been averted in the nineteenth century under the influence of the Missouri Synod, he now felt that the special confessional emphasis of the Missouri Synod had achieved its purpose and that the day had arrived for broader union.

But by the autumn of 1913 Larsen's hope for an understanding with the Missouri Synod had begun to fade. Furthermore, his efforts to approach his old friends in the Missouri Synod were basically resisted and largely unfruitful. His espousal of the union movement had made him *persona non grata* in the eyes of Missouri's leaders. When Larsen passed away in 1915, only a brief note of his passing appeared in the periodical of the Missouri Synod. This was so ironic because Larsen had taught in the Missouri Synod's Concordia Seminary and had been very closely associated with the Missouri Synod most of his life. In addition, in 1903, just twelve years before his death, Larsen had received an honorary doctorate from Concordia Seminary.

*Union Progress*

In 1913 the Synod's extraordinary convention had taken two actions regarding the other church bodies. First, it had adopted the majority report with the understanding that the United Church and Hauge's Synod remove the offending parentheses from paragraph one of the Madison Agreement. This action was to assure the main-liners in the Synod that when they voted for the Madison Agreement, they were voting for a doctrine and not a doctrinal form. In 1913 the United Church sanctioned the removal of the parentheses. Hauge's Synod did not—but that would come later.

Second, the Synod requested the United Church to retract its 1910 judgment of Stub's theses on election. This the United Church refused to do on these grounds: (1) They had never been considered by the church in convention. (2) They had never been published in its official organ. (3) They were unknown to its membership. In other words, since the United Church had never officially expressed itself on Stub's theses, it therefore had never passed "judgment" on them. It would have been a courtesy if the United Church or President Dahl had complied with this request. It would have facilitated good will in the union movement. It should be observed, however, that both the Synod and the United Church did pass resolutions in 1913 absolving the church bodies, as such, of responsibility for unofficial utterances by their members. Nor would they hold other churches responsible for statements of individuals within their bodies. This is noteworthy in view of the "unofficial" attitude within the United Church toward Stub's theses, and the appearance of "The Petition" in the Synod.

Hauge's Synod also did not respond affirmatively to the Synod's request to remove the parentheses in the Madison Agreement. Haugeans reasoned that since Hauge's Synod had not participated in the drafting of the Madison Agreement, it could hardly authorize changes in the documents.

The second meeting of the Joint Union Committee was scheduled for January 21-23, 1914. President Stub feared that this meeting might not be successful in light of the 1913 actions of the United Church and Hauge's Synod—in refusing to comply with Synod requests. Thus President Stub arranged a private meeting with Dr. J. N. Kildahl of the United Church to consider the objections which had been raised against the Madison Agreement. Together they arrived at a statement which was in agreement with the explanation originally proposed at the Synod's Minnesota District convention in 1912.

The second Joint Union Committee meeting was held in Minneapolis, January 21-23, 1914. The Stub-Kildahl declaration was unanimously accepted. Dr. Stub's statesmanship was strongly apparent. A joint resolution warning against unionism, fanaticism, and inter-church cooperation with non-Lutheran Protestants (those holding to confessions differing from the three deliberating bodies) was adopted. Once again, we see the Synod's influence.

This Joint Union Committee meeting then proceeded to name the Committee on Conditions of Union and the Committee on the Constitution of the new merged church body. Dr. Stub would be the convener of the first committee. President Dahl of the United Church would be the convener of the second committee. These two committees were to report in two months at the next Joint Meeting, March 31, 1914. The Joint Committee also considered the issue of synodical institutions and funds. It was decided that all synodical debts be liquidated before the union.

The third Joint Union Committee meeting was held March 31-April 2, 1914. At this meeting the structural framework of the proposed new church was, in the main, constructed. The Joint Committee received the reports of both the Committee on Conditions of Union and the Committee on the Constitution, together with a minority report from the constitution committee. Only the report of the first committee, Conditions of Union, was actually considered at this meeting. The committee presented nineteen articles of union.

Diverse synodical reactions to the articles of union took place in the three general synodical conventions later that year: Hauge's Synod postponed consideration until the proposed constitution was acted on. The United Church, after a lively discussion, adopted them unanimously. The Synod approved them better than two-to-one (68 percent to 32 percent). The actual Synod vote was 360 to 170.

In the Synod General Convention there was lively discussion, indicating strong diversity between the majority and minority. This was the same convention which received the results of the congregational referendum at 95.7 percent approval. Now the convention arranged a "Peace Committee" to report to the 1916 Synod General Convention concerning the action to approve the articles of union. Moreover, the Synod acted to declare the year 1915 a year of cessation of union discussion within its ranks.

It was apparent from the vote to approve (360 to 170), though decisive, that a stronger minority had appeared in the Synod than previously. Obviously, this minority would need to be faced and dealt with. The course toward union would need some problem-solving and some shoring-up. It was not by accident that the convention felt the need to establish a "Peace Committee."

The fourth Joint Union Committee meeting on merger was held April 13-15, 1915. At the beginning of this meeting, Dr. Stub read a statement calling attention to two obstacles to union: The first was the unremoved parentheses in paragraph one of the Madison Agreement. The Synod already had agreed to remove them. The United Church agreed, too—

providing that other bodies did—and Hauge's Synod had refused to do so. Because Hauge's Synod had not done so, the Joint Committee proposed to Hauge's Synod that it agree to the removal. The second obstacle was the unretracted judgment of the United Church committee in 1910 over Stub's theses on election. The Joint Committee resolved to turn this matter over for the separate consideration of the United Church committee members.

The United Church later reported back their refusal to do so on technical grounds: First, the judgment was not spoken by the United Church itself. Second, the Settlement of 1912, by its very nature, annulled all previous articles, judgments, and declarations which contradicted the constituent articles. Technically this may have been correct. However, the United Church committee could have acted out of courtesy and paved the way for better and more positive union negotiations. President Dahl could have personally withdrawn his 1910 statement in the name of mutual harmony.

As it was, the Union Committee of the Synod acted and reported its essential agreement with the interpretation given to the "Settlement" by the United Church committee. The Synod played the bigger role in this small skirmish and more assertively facilitated union harmony.

The remainder of the sessions was devoted to the organizational problems confronting the proposed new church, the proposed new constitution. The constitutional draft was approved for presentation to the three church bodies. The Joint Union Committee meeting was continued into the month of May in order to finalize the proposed name for the new body: "The Norwegian Lutheran Church in America." Thereupon, the Joint Committee adjourned at the call of the synodical presidents.

One interesting sidelight had appeared in 1913: The Synod's English periodical, *Lutheran Herald*, editorialized with the charge of "racialism" because the new name contained the term "Norwegian." This charge was made by its German editor, Pastor Theodore Graebner of the Missouri Synod, when he resigned from the editorship in 1913 in order to accept the call to a professorship at Concordia Seminary in St. Louis.

At the Synod convention in the late spring of 1915, it was clear by previous action that no action would be taken. The Synod had in 1914 declared 1915 a year of cessation of union discussion. Nevertheless, President Stub at the general convention made reference to the union movement by stating that no protests against the action of the previous

1914 convention on the question of union had been received from any of the Synod congregations. Furthermore, Stub read the resolutions prepared by the Joint Union Committee together with the proposed constitution of the new church body.

However, the year 1915 revealed that union was still not a foregone conclusion. At best it seemed probable that a minority in the Synod would remain opposed to the union cause. Such a minority existed in Hauge's Synod, too.

## Final Steps Toward Merger

By 1916 the Synod was prepared to take action to consummate the merger with the United Church, with or without Hauge's Synod. There was real concern that the Hauge minority could prevent Hauge's Synod from entering the union. However, the Synod took decisive action to insure the merger. In the process the minority in the Synod became more high-profile and more resolute.

The church council called an extraordinary convention in 1916 (it was not a normal convention year) to deliberate the question of union. The convention met May 18-24 in Minneapolis. The Peace Committee of 1914 had been deadlocked and was unable to report a reconciliation. The real test at the convention was the three enabling acts, prepared by the Joint Union Committee's attorney, which would guarantee the Union. These were as follows—along with Synod action on each one:

1) Final adoption of all previously-ratified documents. The Synod convention vote was 522 to 202 (or 72 percent approval).
2) Consummation of the actual merger of the three church bodies. The Synod convention vote was 491 to 187 (or 72.4 percent approval).
3) Transfer of all synodical properties to the new church body. The Synod convention vote was 482 to 181 (or 72.6 percent approval).

The main business of the convention was completed. But hope for reconciliation disappeared in the concluding discussion on the union. Pastor N. N. Boe presented a motion that the church council and all church officers, pastors, and professors loyally support the resolutions of the Synod. He explained that the purpose of his motion was to assure peace and to allow the church council to see to it that the decisions of the Synod Convention and church council would be carried out by each and every member.

At this point Pastor I. B. Torrison of First Lutheran Church in Decorah immediately presented a statement which bore the signatures of 176 men. (This was about the same number who in 1914 had voted against the articles of union.) This statement requested the Synod to advise the other church bodies that only the acceptance of the minority's views would make possible the entrance of this group into the merger. To deny this resolution, the minority declared, would lead to a break in the Synod

Boe's motion was adopted, and the motions to implement the Torrison resolution were laid on the table. With this, it was clear that the feelings of the minority would quickly crystallize into action.

## *The Synod Minority Continues Opposition*

The minority group within the Synod numbered 170 and 176 at the 1914 and 1916 Synod conventions respectively. Obviously this group was large enough that they could not be ignored. The minority claimed that they had tried to engage with the Synod leadership for some time—presumably between the 1914 and 1916 conventions, or before. They claimed that they had been ignored and/or were unable to enter into serious discussion with the leadership. In any event, there was a stalemate. Thus the 1916 Synod convention and the presentation to the convention of the statement which bore 176 names was a breaking point for them.

Basically, the minority was taking exception to the Madison Agreement/Settlement of 1912; they wished to have it revised in crucial ways which we will not review here. It does not appear that, as a group, the minority was strongly opposed to the union, but they strongly wished for a change of conditions.

In many respects, the minority represented the traditional mainline position of the Synod. The Synod had always promoted union negotiations, but always along strongly confessional lines. Without doubt, the minority was being strongly influenced by the Missouri Synod's criticism of the Madison Agreement/Settlement of 1912 and further union negotiations. They considered many of the Missouri Synod persons making these criticisms to be their close friends. The final actions of the 1916 Synod convention in approving the union had left the minority feeling rebuffed and isolated. Complicating their position—most minority persons were pastors—was the strong laity support for the union, including most members of their own parishes.

*Leadership Works to Satisfy Minority Group*

Knowledge of these circumstances led two leaders in the United Church to conclude that the leaders of the minority might still be open to the union movement. With this in mind, Dr. J. N. Kildahl and Dr. L. W. Boe, of the United Church, got in touch with President C. K. Preus of Luther College and Pastor I. B. Torrison of First Lutheran Church in Decorah. (This was help being offered from a different and unexpected source.) Kildahl and Boe raised the question whether they might conceivably be of some help in solving the stalemate which now threatened to split the Synod on the eve of the proposed union.

To this Preus and Torrison responded by extending a cordial invitation to Kildahl and Boe to come to Decorah and discuss the whole matter. The invitation was accepted. The conversations were carried on informally and in a frank and friendly spirit. The friendship which had existed between Dr. Kildahl and Pastor Torrison since college days, when they were classmates and fast friends at Luther College, contributed to the fine spirit which pervaded the discussions. The conversations resulted in a joint statement which met the request of the minority on the controversial points.

On October 4, 1916, the statement was immediately forwarded to the Joint Union Committee, which considered it at its October 12 meeting. For technical reasons the committee found itself unable to recommend the statement for adoption by the three respective church bodies which were to meet in June 1917. It was the feeling of the Committee that it might cause "misunderstandings, difficulties, and tensions."

The action taken by the Joint Union Committee prompted Kildahl, Boe, Torrison, and Preus to hold a second meeting, this time in Austin, Minnesota. The statement agreed upon in Decorah was reviewed and revised so as to meet the objections of the Joint Union Committee. This revised statement came to be known as the Austin Agreement. It was re-submitted to the Joint Union Committee at its December 5-7 meeting, which made the following recommendations for adoption by the 1917 general conventions of the three respective church bodies:

> The annual meeting expressly takes cognizance of the three reservations concerning sections 1, 3, and 4 in the Madison Agreement as stated in the request of Professor C. K. Preus and the Rev. I. B. Torrison and declares that there is nothing in the above-mentioned request which is contrary to Scrip-

ture and the Confessions, and that we regard the positions taken in that document are sufficient expression of unity of faith. Therefore that group of men and congregations whose position is stated in the above cited request are invited to become members of the new body with full equality and mutual brotherly recognition.

Following this action of the Joint Union Committee, Preus and Torrison, in consultation with other minority leaders, called a meeting of all pastors of the minority group in the Old West Hotel in Minneapolis on January 17-18, 1917. In preparation for this meeting, Torrison and Preus decided to make a trip to St. Louis for the purpose of consulting their friends in the Missouri Synod. They met with Professors Pieper, Dau, and Graebner of Concordia Theological Seminary.

On December 28, 1916, Preus and Torrison met for five hours in the old faculty room at Concordia with these three theological professors. In addition to the 1912 Madison Agreement, with which the professors were already acquainted, the pastors laid before the professors the two essential documents: the Austin Agreement and the resolution of the Joint Union Committee containing the invitation to the minority to "become members of the new body with full equality and mutual brotherly recognition." Then the crucial question was submitted: "Whether we, instead of separating and forming a separate body could, on the strength of the concessions made to us in the Austin Agreement, join the new body?" At the end of the five-hour conference the professors' answer was in the affirmative. Both Torrison and Preus were elated and went on their way rejoicing.

However, when the Concordia professors put their answer/statement in writing, it was quite another story. They used the old trick of addressing and answering a different question than the one that had been asked. In their written statement the Concordia professors dealt with this different question: "Whether the time had come for the minority to leave the Norwegian Synod?" This was not the question which Torrison and Preus had asked; it was not the question dealt with and answered in the five-man, five-hour conference in the old faculty room.

This written reply made the meeting on January 17-18 with the minority group, where just over 100 attended, very difficult for Torrison and Preus. One deplorable result of the written report was the charge made by a few minority men that Preus and Torrison had not reported correctly the advice given by the St. Louis professors. A few were not satisfied with the Austin Agreement. But the great majority of those attending the January 17-18 meeting voted approval of the Austin Agreement. This paved the way for the minority to enter the Union without compromising their convictions. Thus the larger part of the minority—by far—would enter the proposed Union.

Sadly, we must observe that the Synod's friends in the Missouri Synod had not served them well. In fact, it was a double cross. Both the Synod majority (via President Stub) in 1912 and now the Synod minority (via Professor Preus and Pastor Torrison) in 1916 had attempted to keep faith with Missouri. In both cases they were let down very significantly. It was, in both instances, a betrayal.

Eventually the conversations in St. Louis with Torrison and Preus and the Concordia professors would be clarified and vindicated. But it would not take place until twenty-one years later in 1938. By that time several of those involved would have entered eternal rest—including Preus and Torrison. One living professor finally set the record straight. Then it would be another twenty years, in 1958, before this clarification and vindication would be fully recorded in writing.

## The Joint Union Committee's Final Meetings and Actions

Between the regular general conventions of the three church bodies in 1916 and 1917, the Joint Union Committee held five formal meetings, totaling twenty-eight days in session. These meetings covered eight months (October 1916 through May 1917). The committee's duties were broad in scope and detailed in nature. Among the many tasks and accomplishments during the final days of the Union Committee's meeting, it provided an agenda for the constituting convention of the Norwegian Lutheran Church in America (NLCA). It also provided a plan for the equitable distribution of official positions among representatives of the three uniting church bodies.

## Union Is Completed

The Synod readily and happily gave up its separate existence in the Grand Union in order that it might be continued in the new merged church body with fellow Lutherans of Norwegian background. It wrapped up its separate existence June 6-8, 1917, in convention assembled, in St. Paul.

The new Norwegian Lutheran Church in America (NLCA) met in constituting convention in the days that immediately followed in the St. Paul Auditorium. Synod President Dr. H. G. Stub was elected general president of the new NLCA at this constituting convention.

CHAPTER SEVENTEEN

# An Evaluation of The Norwegian Synod

A great many threads went into weaving the fabric of the Norwegian Synod. German confessional Lutheranism was an extremely strong and almost inflexible strand; this thread was in reaction to the rampant European theological rationalism of that period. Of equal importance was the strong Norwegian conservatism of their heritage, which was moderately tinged with pietism.

As the German type of pious orthodoxy came to Norway (through theological professors Johnson and Caspari), the hold of Danish theology (then prevalent in Norway) waned. The Johnsonian awakening was momentous not only for Norway but for the Synod and the other Norwegian-American church bodies as well. This theological awakening united orthodoxy with clear evangelical preaching. It is clear now (in retrospect) that the Lutheranism transplanted from Norway to the great American Midwest was a blending of the most vigorous types of Lutheranism which Europe had to offer. Theological aberrations and extremes of the several varieties current in nineteenth century Europe were largely avoided. The Synod pastors and leaders depended basically on standard Lutheran authorities.

The problems of Europe were not the problems of the American Midwest frontier. The problems of the frontier were basically the age-old enemies of vital Christian faith. One such enemy was indifferentism, which prevailed among many of the Norwegian immigrants. Indifferentism was present among the Norwegians, even though they came from a country which had just been deeply touched by a great spiritual awakening—led by lay evangelist Hans Nielsen Hauge and theological professor Gisle Johnson.

The problems faced by these young and vigorous Synod pastors (most were in their twenties and early thirties) were the problems of the frontier: distance, comparative poverty, and lack of experience. These were not the problems of Europe for which they had been educated and prepared, but these problems and difficulties challenged their scattered flocks.

The leaders of the Synod were strong (and often misunderstood) men. In their problems they recognized opportunities, and in their difficulties they saw a supreme challenge. When rivers and swamps separated them from their people, they simply crossed them. When a complacent state Church of Norway failed to see its moral obligation to its members who had emigrated from the homeland to the United States, these Synod leaders simply rose to the occasion.. They wasted little time in recrimination. Instead they took uncertain and bold steps which lead to the building of an indigenous church (the Synod). Confident in the knowledge that their God preferred errors in judgment to indolence and self-pitying inactivity, they set forth on projects which cool calculation should have ruled out altogether.

Their Lutheranism was of such a strenuous confessionalism and awareness of their heritage that it proved impossible for them to be absorbed into a melting-pot Protestantism. It is well to note that the heightened confessional spirit of the Synod's pastors and leaders needed to be attributed to the fact that they were their own theologians. Their background was important, but their writings and their sermons indicate that they personally chose the strongly confessional Lutheran path. It is clear that their robust confessional orthodoxy was re-invigorated and strongly supported by their self-chosen affiliation with the Missouri Synod. It was the Missouri Synod affiliation which infused new vigor and assurance into pastors and leaders already convinced of the essential rightness of their historic Lutheranism. Affinity existed before affiliation.

In this process Professor C. F. W. Walther, the leader of the Missouri Synod, became a leader and dominant figure in the Norwegian Synod. For three full decades Walther was as influential in the Synod as any Synod pastor/leader. It seems apparent, however, that even the strong men of the Synod leaned too often and too heavily on Walther. The doubts and suspicions of a few of the pastors and many of the laymen regarding an undue dependence on Missouri were to some degree justified.

Whether Professor Walther, who knew his own people so well, knew the Norwegians and their needs well enough, may be doubted. He could not (or did not) sense that at many points the position of his beloved Norwegian brethren was significantly different from his own German brothers. The German Missourians had come to America on a community pilgrimage from Saxony. The Synod's background was far more diverse. The Synod's task was not so much one of working out from within a recognized center and power of evangelism, it was rather that of gathering individuals and small groups into a body (Synod) which was at first amorphous. What was effective churchmanship in St. Louis did not fit the needs of scattered Norwegian settlers. The Norwegians had migrated for an entirely different set of reasons.

It could also be argued that the Missourian Germans and the Synod Norwegians had two different sets of mind, both a product of their homeland's peculiar history. When the strong leaders of the Synod attempted to follow Walther's clear and theoretically brilliant counsel, they frequently encountered resistance born of Norwegian individualism. This individualism and independence dated not only from the 1814 independence of Norway, but from the emergence of that European stock which could and did produce the wandering and fierce Vikings.

If it was unfortunate, as many have suggested, that the Synod allied itself both practically and theologically with Missouri, the misfortune seems to be psychological rather than theological. Just as the Norwegian European churchmen could not sense the deepest needs and problems of their migrated American children, so Walther could not sense that the Norwegians were not his Germans. Arguably, the slavery issue and the Election Controversy were the flash-points at which Professor Walther and the Missouri Synod misled the Norwegian Synod.

At the same time, it must be noted that the Synod's leaders were, on their part, not sufficiently sensitive to the spirit of their own people. Nor were they sufficiently able to realize that they tended toward a rigorous and theological purism which their people were unable to share or appreciate. Their spirit has been interpreted by such words as "doctrinaire," "arrogant," and "exclusive." More charitably, their weakness may be seen as a failure to realize that their spiritual children could be given more freedom without compromising fundamental doctrines or deep Christian convictions.

Only rarely is the ethos of militant orthodoxy given either a sympathetic or fully charitable appraisal. Critics usually judge it not by its best elements, but by what seems to be its worst. The Synod deserves a sympathetic interpretation which takes into account not only its visible and institutional contributions, but also its less tangible contribution to the spirit and theology of a Lutheranism still in process on the American scene.

One-sided, perhaps, was the synod's insistence on theological principles, which relate it closely to the "genuine Lutherans" of another century and continent. Though one-sided, it was also necessary. Without the theological stringency and ardent confessionalism which characterized the Synod, Norwegian Lutheranism in the United States might well have fumbled its way to a position in which the name "Lutheran" would have become a nostalgic label rather than a title conveying theological meaning.

To insist on this is not to disavow the various contributions of other groups of Norwegian Lutherans. Each group had its own peculiar strengths and made its best efforts to convey living Christianity to the frontier settlers. No one church body had a monopoly on truth or an infallible sense of what was best for the immigrants. Yet the Norwegian Synod, while its years as an independent organization were numbered, brought strength, vigor, and theological steadfastness to a land where religious chaos reigned and might well have overcome the Norwegian immigrants.

Woven firmly into the fabric of today's American Lutheranism is the strong stand of the old Norwegian Synod.

# APPENDIX

# Synod Membership

The records show steady growth of the Synod during its years in existence—except for one major disruption. The following are some statistics, which illustrate its growth:

At the Synod's founding (1853)
  Pastors: 7
  Congregations: 38
  Membership: 11,400 (estimated)

By 1870 the total membership had grown to approximately 80,000.

At the Synod's silver jubilee (twenty-fifth anniversary) in 1878
  Pastors: 137
  Congregations: 570
  Membership: 124,367

At the climax of the Election Controversy
  Membership before the controversy: 144,000 (1887)
  Lost in the Controversy: 50,000
  Membership following the controversy: 94,000 (1890)

By the Synod's golden jubilee (fiftieth anniversary) in 1903 the Synod had recouped its Election Controversy losses. Once again the membership was 144,000.

Unofficial statistics in 1915
  Pastors: 410
  Congregations: 1,048
  Membership: 162,287

Official statistics in 1916, the last parochial report before the Grand Union
  Pastors: 362
  Membership: 160,547
  Confirmed Membership: 96,905

By 1917, in spite of the Election Controversy, the Synod was almost exactly twice as large as it had been in 1870.

# Sources

Information in the book is based in large measure on the following sources:

**Chapter One: The False Start and the Bona Fide Start**
J. C. K. Preus, ed., *Norsemen Found a Church* (Minneapolis: Augsburg Publishing House, 1953), Chapter 7 titled "The Making of a Constitution" by E. Clifford Nelson, 191-222. E. Clifford Nelson and Eugene L. Fevold, *The Lutheran Church Among Norwegian-Americans* (Minneapolis: Augsburg Publishing House, 1960), vol. I, 152-158.

**Chapter Two: The Immediate History of the Synod Following Organization**
Nelson and Fevold, vol. I, 61-168 and 245-246; and J. Magnus Rohne, *Norwegian-American Lutheranism Up To 1872* (New York: The Macmillan Company, 1926) on the Synod's doctrinal clarifications: "The Church," 149-150; "Lay Activity," 164-168; "The Sunday Question," 223-226; "Absolution," 227-233; "Justification," 233-240.

**Chapter Three: Founding Pastors of the Synod**
Gerhard L. Belgum, *The Old Norwegian Synod in America 1853-1890* (New Haven, Connecticut: Yale University, 1957), 219-237. An unpublished doctoral dissertation.

**Chapter Four: The Polity of the Synod Revised**
Nelson and Fevold, vol. I, 180-182.

**Chapter Five: Membership in the Synodical Conference**
Nelson and Fevold, vol. I, 182-183.

**Chapter Six: The Slavery Issue**
David T. Nelson, *Luther College 1861-1961* (Decorah, Iowa: Luther College Press, 1961), 75-88. The observations at the end of Chapter Six are entirely those of the author/editor.

**Chapter Seven: Inter-Synodical Theological Discussion**
Nelson and Fevold, vol. I, 241-270.

**Chapter Eight: Publications**
Preus, Chapter 14 ("Tell It to the People—Publications" by O. G. Malmin and Fernanda Urberg Malmin), 389-406.

**Chapter Nine: Worship and Church Music**
Preus, Chapter 13 ("The Heritage of Music" by Laurence N. Field), 379-388.

**Chapter Ten: The Election Controversy**
A. Nelson and Fevold, vol. I, 258-270; and Joseph M. Shaw, *Bernt Julius Muus* (Northfield, Minnesota: Norwegian-American Historical Association, 1999), 307-334. The introduction, the alerts, and the conclusion are entirely those of the author/editor.

**Chapter Eleven: Home Missions Before the Election Controversy**
Nelson and Fevold, vol. I, 271-282.

**Chapter Twelve: Home Missions Following the Election Controversy**
Nelson and Fevold, vol. II, 85-103.

**Chapter Thirteen: The Synod's Education Enterprise**
David T. Nelson, *Luther College 1861-1961*; Nelson and Fevold, vol. II, 112-121; Preus, Chapter 10 ("Holding High the Torch" by Lydia Bredesen Sundby), 293-325; and Shaw, Chapter 10 ("The Founding of St. Olaf College"), 233-256.

**Chapter Fourteen: The Synod and Foreign Missions**
Nelson and Fevold, vol. II, 103-108; Preus, Chapter 11 ("Burning Zeal—Mission Endeavor" by Andrew S. Burgess), 329-361.

**Chapter Fifteen: Charitable Institutions**
Nelson and Fevold, vol. II, 108-112; Preus, Chapter 15 ("They Had Compassion" by Magnus A. Dahlen), 407-417.

**Chapter Sixteen: The Union Movement in the Synod**
Rohne, 125-126; Gustav M. Bruce, ed., *The Union Documents of the Evangelical Lutheran Church* (Minneapolis, 1948), especially Part I ("A Brief Historical Survey of the Union Movement"), 1-27; Nelson and Fevold, vol. II, 129-225; J. C. K. Preus, *The Union Movement and the "Minority," 1917* (Minneapolis, 1958).

**Chapter Seventeen: An Evaluation of the Synod**
Gerhard L. Belgum, 419-426.

**Appendix**
Belgum, 415; Knut Gjerset, *History of the Norwegian People* (New York: The Macmillan Company, 1915), vol. II, 609; Bruce, 3 (dealing with parochial reports).

# Bibliography

Belgum, Gerhard L. *The Old Norwegian Synod in America 1853-1890*. New Haven, Connecticut: Yale University, 1957. Unpublished doctoral dissertation.

Bjork, Kenneth O. *West of the Great Divide: Norwegian Migration to the West Coast, 1847-1898*. Northfield, Minnesota: Norwegian-American Historical Association, 1958.

Bruce, Gustav M., ed. *The Union Documents of the Evangelical Lutheran Church: With a Historical Survey of the Union Movement*. Minneapolis, Minnesota, 1948.

Gjerset, Knut. *History of the Norwegian People*. Volumes I and II. New York: The Macmillan Company, 1915.

Larsen, Karen. *Laur. Larsen: Pioneer College President*. Northfield, Minnesota: Norwegian-American Historical Association, 1936.

Lueker, Erwin L. *Lutheran Cyclopedia*. St. Louis, Missouri: Concordia Publishing House, 1954.

Nelson, David T., translator and editor. *The Diary of Elizabeth Koren 1853-1855*. Northfield, Minnesota: Norwegian-American Historical Association, 1955.

Nelson, David T. *Luther College 1861-1961*. Decorah, Iowa: Luther College Press, 1961.

Nelson, E. Clifford, and Eugene L. Fevold. *The Lutheran Church Among Norwegian-Americans: A History of the Evangelical Lutheran Church*. Volumes I and II. Minneapolis, Minnesota: Augsburg Publishing House, 1960.

Preus, J. C. K. *A Critical Look: A Critical Look at The Lutheran Church Among Norwegian-Americans by Professors E. Clifford Nelson and Eugene L. Fevold of Luther Theological Seminary, St. Paul, Minnesota.* Minneapolis, Minnesota, 1978. Copyrighted but not published.

Preus, J. C. K., ed. *Norsemen Found a Church: An Old Heritage in a New Land.* Minneapolis, Minnesota: Augsburg Publishing House, 1953.

Preus, J. C. K. *The Union Movement and the "Minority," 1917.* Minneapolis, Minnesota, 1958. Copyrighted but not published.

Rohne, J. Magnus. *Norwegian American Lutheranism Up To 1872.* New York: The Macmillan Company, 1926.

Shaw, Joseph M. *Bernt Julius Muus: Founder of St. Olaf College.* Northfield, Minnesota: Norwegian-American Historical Association, 1999.

Slind, Marvin G., translator and editor, and Gracia Grindal, sketch editor. *Linka's Diary: A Norwegian Immigrant Story in Word and Sketches.* Minneapolis, Minnesota: Lutheran University Press, 2008.

Tappert, Theodore G., editor. *The Book of Concord: The Confessions of the Evangelical Lutheran Church.* Philadelphia, Pennsylvania: Fortress Press, 1959.

Wee, Mons. *Haugeanism.* Minneapolis, Minnesota, 1918. Privately published.

www.ingramcontent.com/pod-product-compliance
Lightning Source LLC
Chambersburg PA
CBHW050321120526
44592CB00014B/1997